A trained journalist, Helen Jacobs was a successful PR and marketing executive who left her thriving career to become a full-time psychic, hosting popular workshops and events to provide thousands of readings for people all over the world. In addition to her work as a medium, Helen mentors and teaches women how to change their lives and find a more meaningful path for themselves. She is the author of *You Already Know: How to access your intuition and find your divine life path* and *Asking for a Friend: Answers from the Universe to life's big questions.*

FOLLOW YOUR HEART

Simple daily rituals for honing your intuition

HELEN JACOBS

affirm
press

First published by Affirm Press in 2023
Boon Wurrung Country
28 Thistlethwaite Street
South Melbourne VIC 3205
affirmpress.com.au

10 9 8 7 6 5 4 3 2 1

A catalogue record for this
book is available from the
National Library of Australia

ISBN: 9781922863409 (hardback)

Cover design by Alissa Dinallo © Affirm Press
Typeset in 11.5/15.5 pt Baskerville by Post Pre-press Group
Printed and bound in China by C&C Offset Printing

For all those courageous enough
to follow the beat of their own heart.

CONTENTS

INTRODUCTION

'Have the courage to follow your heart and intuition. They somehow already know what you truly want to become,' Steve Jobs famously advised during his commencement address to Stanford students in 2005. When one of the world's wealthiest and arguably most influential people gives this life advice, you may be inclined to pay attention. With more than 40 million views of his address on YouTube, it's safe to assume his advice hits upon something we instinctively resonate with, but perhaps don't logically understand how to do. Following his advice, let alone your heart and intuition, is not necessarily as easy as Steve made it seem.

While preparing to write this book, I asked my Instagram community if they could articulate what they truly desired, deep in their heart. Not their emotions or romantic rumblings, but instead, could they identify what they *really* wanted at their deepest, truest core. What about you? What do your heart and intuition desire most right now?

I then asked my community, as I'll ask you now, assuming you do know what your heart wants, do you know how to make it happen? Will you follow your heart's desire, or calling or yearning – even if it doesn't make sense or is risky, scary or impractical? Do you believe manifesting your heart-led desire is possible or, more importantly, possible *for you*?

The feedback mirrored what I've seen in my private practice with clients for the past fifteen years. Some respondents could clearly articulate their heart's desire, but the vast majority could not. Most were loosely familiar with the principles of manifesting, but also struggled to put it into practice. Time and time again, I've seen people just like you yearning to live rich, meaningful and fulfilling lives, but feeling conflicted about their desires, about how to fulfil their dreams in a way that feels good to them while also trying to placate those around them. This appears to be particularly true for the many women I've worked with. Women are acutely attuned to others' desires for them, whether that's their spouse, children, parents, bosses, colleagues, social media, neighbours, siblings – just about *everyone* else's expectations rate a mention, often more than their own heart.

Following my heart was so transformative that I dedicated the past fifteen years to fine-tuning the process and teaching others how to do the same. This very book exists because I followed my heart. Following a random, sudden urge one Tuesday afternoon, I reached out to say hello to my publisher and, by the end of our brief conversation, this book was imagined and a few days later it was commissioned. Acting on such simple intuitive prompts has helped me achieve my heart's deepest dreams. My heart has no interest in replicating Steve's success, but I have followed my inner knowing to buy and sell houses, to marry my husband and start our family, to grow my business and more. My clients have fulfilled their own humble, heartfelt dreams by being courageous enough to try.

At age twenty-seven, I took my first big leap to follow my heart and intuition out of my job as the Australian and New Zealand public relations manager for a leading online travel company – to become a *psychic*. (Yes, it surprised me too.) I shared this journey in my first book, *You Already Know*. Leaving my PR job, I began giving psychic readings mainly out of curiosity. Following my heart (and a little higher guidance from the world of spirit), what began as card readings at my kitchen table has become a fully-fledged online business, serving thousands of people the world over. As time went on, and as I shared in my last book, *Asking For a Friend*, I became less interested in accessing guidance on my clients' behalf and far more interested in teaching and supporting them to trust themselves, their heart and intuition. You are now about to join their ranks.

Yes, everyone is intuitive. Even you. Following the heart's inner wisdom isn't widely taught, let alone encouraged, perhaps because it's often inconvenient to those around us if we have a mind, or more accurately a heart, of our own. Despite being able to access guidance beyond what I physically see and touch, I'm always brought back to the truth of my own heart, the deep knowing of my body and the way life rushes in to support me when I ask. You're about to learn how the simple act of asking for what you want (once you know what that really is) opens the floodgates to an abundance of aligned opportunities – if you let it.

Why Follow Your Heart?

Accessing your intuition and trusting your heart's lead helps you create your dream life – one full of authenticity and meaning. Through simple, small daily steps, built upon weekly and then monthly, you'll be gently guided out of your head and back into your heart, the home of your inner knowing. There, you'll reconnect with your heart's desires and learn to follow where they lead you. Tuning into your heart's deepest desires is as much about what you *don't* want as it is what you're ready to heal, to process and manifest next. Your inner knowing is that powerful. Fine-tuning your heart to receive the Universe's messages, while also transmitting your own requests, catalyses a powerful feedback loop, one rich with intuitive guidance.

Chances are, your heart is already trying to get your attention. All too often, hunches, feelings, or strange 'knowings' are ignored. We can't explain them, there's no 'good' reason for them – and yet ignoring these niggling feelings only turns those gentle inner whispers into massive clangs about the head. That niggle to change jobs or end that relationship or make some other change soon becomes a full-blown problem and you *just knew* you should have acted on that hunch when it first showed up. Yeah, that's your heart trying to get your attention.

Don't feel like you've experienced such Universal whispers or inner nudges? Don't be disheartened. Perhaps you fall into the ever-growing chorus of people completely consumed by the relentless noise of our fast-paced world. Amid the noise and confusion of our busy lives, your heart may have been drowned out. This book is most certainly also for you.

How to Use This Book

Heads up: this is a book where you actually need to participate. It's written as a mini program, so you'll get the most out of it by putting something in (and you'll soon see how the Universe rewards this). Please attempt the exercises as you reach them. You'll need a journal on hand for this. Experiment with these exercises so that by the end of each chapter your heart can personalise the ritual.

With love, I now gently say: if you can't follow your heart here, I would argue you probably won't follow it with more high-risk decisions either. Any resistance you feel towards the exercises, even the way your head says, 'Oh, just read it, do it in your head, you can come back to it later', is important data! It's proof your head will fight to stay in control. We'll soon explore how to balance your head and heart, but until then, please do your heart a favour and actually do the exercises, ok?

Each chapter and its exercises build on the previous ones. Starting with exploring the role of the head and heart, you'll learn the link between intuition and manifesting, working with a process for asking the Universe for what you want, and actually receiving it. Moving from the process to the tools, you'll build your daily ritual before expanding it into weekly and monthly practices, too – and beyond! By the end of the book, you'll have tailored your practice to attune to your heart's desires, transmit them to the Universe, and receive the Universe's guidance and support to make it happen.

Getting Started

First, a few practicalities:

- ♥ Put aside at least a few minutes a day to work with this book and follow the practices.

- ♥ You'll need a journal and pen to get started.

- ♥ You might like to visit helenjacobs.co for additional tools to support this process.

Now, for the only thing you truly need. And it's right there, in the first line of the book in Steve's now famous words. You've got to have the *courage* to follow your heart and intuition. If you can muster up the courage, I'll help you figure out the rest.

PART ONE

THE METHOD

CHAPTER ONE

THE HEART IS
AN ANTENNA

Do you believe life is geared in your favour? Your answer to this question could greatly influence your ability to receive guidance and manifest accordingly. Belief in this possibility is pivotal. If you believe that, yes, life is geared in your favour, manifesting and receiving guidance will be all that much easier. If you believe it is not, then your resistance will be met by more Universal resistance.

Of course, the idea that life is working for you is more difficult to swallow when all evidence to date feels to the contrary. Our challenges, personal and collective, can indeed make it feel like the world is against us. I admit, I used to believe the world was against me (and from time to time, this idea can creep back in – that's normal). Early in my professional psychic life though, I realised **life isn't just geared in my favour, *life is actively working with me to succeed.*** This was totally revolutionary at the time. As I pursued my new calling, I began to see that life's challenges have more to do with our lessons than any proof the Universe is stacked against us. Even the challenges are working for us, helping us grow and catalyse change – but we may need to flip our thinking.

Logic will fight hard against this premise, but the Universe will carry on operating outside the bounds of logic anyway. Observing and experimenting with the Universe's illogical ways, a world of intuitive data, insight and *proof* will be gathered. This concept actually works – but not how our minds expect it to. Working with these principles is less about asking for a lottery win or manipulating favourable outcomes and more about self-awareness and personal growth. It's about receiving what is intended for us, and becoming who we are meant to be, according to our own hearts.

Whether we're asking for guidance or manifesting our best life, the Universe is listening and responding. How we ask is as important as how we receive the response. **We can apply the same formula for manifesting opportunities to manifest solutions, answers and guidance.** The technique is the same no matter what we ask for, but our results will depend on the belief and intention with which the request is made.

A fine line separates working *with* the Universe and absolving our personal power to it. We most certainly have a role to play here; our choice and free will is paramount. We cannot leave everything to chance or squarely in the Universe's hands by simply 'going with the flow' and hoping for the best. Knowing our heart's desire *and* harnessing the Universe's magic to make it happen, life can – and will – dramatically change.

Still unsure? Could you at least be *willing* to believe life is geared in your favour? *Willingness* initiates a new vibration and, without you even doing anything else just yet, that vibration of willingness can change your results, just like the courage you mustered in the last chapter. But if you stay closed, so will the Universe.

It's (Universal) Law

This isn't just some fanciful idea or positive platitudes; it's based on Universal Law. The Law of Attraction, the poster child of Universal Laws, may have gained notoriety but it doesn't work alone. When all the Universal Laws are understood and applied, the full backing of the Universe is behind the life you want to create, supporting you in following your heart.

Universal Laws are the silent but potent forces at play governing how life works. Without them, your manifesting and guidance is incomplete. Working with them, your dreams take on depth, meaning and possibility. These laws explain how to communicate with the Universe, how life can flow more easily, how to gracefully grow and change, showing you that what you put into life will be returned to you. But it all happens outside the realm of logic – the Universe is all about the vibe. When you understand how to use your heart to communicate with the Universe by exchanging vibrations, you'll be guided to change internally to receive what you want externally. Because of these laws, you are in a constant vibrational feedback loop with the Universe – and it holds a great deal for you. But before we jump into that feedback loop, let me introduce you to twelve Universal Laws.

THE TWELVE UNIVERSAL LAWS

Law of Divine Oneness: As a result of creation, everything is connected. Every atom of our being is connected to the atoms of every other being. All of life shares a collective source and a collective consciousness.

Law of Vibration: Everything is made of energy – all matter, all living things. Even your thoughts and feelings are energy. Because energy is in constant motion, it vibrates at its own speed, creating its own unique frequency.

Law of Attraction: Like attracts like, especially vibrations. Adjusting your frequency will affect who or what you 'vibe' with (and you can adjust your frequency by changing your thoughts and beliefs).

Law of Correspondence: What occurs within, occurs outside. What happens above, happens below. Your inner world (your thoughts, beliefs, energy) corresponds to your outer world (like your job, money, relationships). Changing one will change the other.

Law of Inspired Action: Without action, there is no change. When the action is inspired, or aligned to the creative source or divine connectedness, you'll feel this in your true heart. Your intuition, Universal signs and heartfelt guidance shows you the Inspired Action to take.

Law of Perpetual Transmutation of Energy: Energy cannot be created or destroyed; it just changes form. Energy is always in motion, evolving from one frequency to another. The energy of our thoughts can be transformed into physical form with Inspired Action.

Law of Cause and Effect: All actions have a reaction, whether positive or negative, whether immediate or delayed, whether known or unknown. Everything is connected through Divine Oneness, even the impacts of our actions.

Law of Compensation: The Universe will return in kind what you contribute, whether positive or negative, a little or a lot. This is a return of energy in your direction for the frequency of energy given out. The return isn't always physical.

Law of Relativity: We are inclined to look at things from our particular perspective, assigning meaning or value to things, but in reality, everything is neutral. The meaning and value assigned is relative to the perception of whoever is perceiving it. You can change your perception and therefore the meaning and value of who and what is before you.

Law of Polarity: Everything has its opposite: positive and negative, light and dark, happy and sad. We cannot only attract one of the poles, we need both and must allow a balance and harmony between the two. Both coexist.

Law of Rhythm: All of life is in constant, effortless motion and fluidity, at a rhythm and speed all of its own. Everything will change, eventually, and cycle back again – even your thoughts and experiences.

Law of Balance: There must be an exchange, a give and take to all things, so a certain balance can be achieved. For life to flow, things must come and go in a state of equilibrium.

The Feedback Loop

Via these Universal Laws, we are in a constant state of vibrational communication with the Universe. Life is working for us, it wants us to succeed, and it's always responding. Listening to our heart, we will *feel* the frequency of our desires, our hopes and dreams. Focusing on the vibration of our desires and taking Inspired Action (via our intuition) towards our desires, we feed into a vibrational exchange with the Universe. The Universe returns serve, bringing us the people, opportunities and situations that are a vibrational match, or highlighting where we need to adjust.

Universal feedback is *mirrored in the answers, situations, relationships and opportunities around you.* A situation that feels confusing, murky or strange hints that something is 'off' internally – we need to alter our vibration. A situation that is flowing, feels great and full of possibility signals a vibrational match. Congratulations! You've manifested your heart's desire (until a new desire comes along and things start to feel 'off' again).

The feedback loop leads to enhanced self-awareness. Receiving feedback from your outer world (your job, relationships, bank account etc.), you know to turn inward to realign your heart, desires, beliefs, energy and actions. Life is showing you where the inner and outer vibrations meet, or need to adjust to create buoyancy. When life's curveballs come your way – and they will – you will see it as an opportunity to refine your energy, let go of something that wasn't working, or look at it through the lens of understanding and advancing your personal growth. All things work for your expansion, or perpetual transmutation of energy.

This Universal feedback loop *is* the guidance; your heart continually processes it, fine-tuning its desires and your internal state, resulting in manifestation or feedback for further fine-tuning.

The Guidance Cycle

How exactly do you adjust your vibration? Well, that's a great question, and one the Universe is better placed to answer! The vibrational feedback from the Universe actually tells you the actions required to alter the vibration. Over time, I observed that the feedback typically points towards something in your inner world that needs to be cleared, healed, restored or manifested (or created). The feedback is continually moving us through this cycle of clearing, healing, restoring and manifesting (what I call the Guidance Cycle) so that we heal and adjust internally to have it appear in our outer world (the Law of Correspondence). Life will continually guide us to make the changes that will allow us to come back to our natural, high-vibing selves.

According to the Law of Rhythm and the Law of Perpetual Transmutation of Energy, our frequency will ebb and flow at a pace all of its own; **we're not meant to be high-vibing all the time.** Besides, the Law of Polarity says we need both the ebb and the flow. Life happens, we respond. And your frequency frequently changes in response to your interactions with the world.

A build-up of lower-vibing experiences, relationships and exchanges will lead to a build-up of lower-vibrational frequencies in our systems – and the feedback loop will show us it's time to release, clear, heal and move on because it feels stuck, stagnant or stationary. We'll go deeper with this idea of raising our vibration through inner work throughout the book. For now, the process of asking the Universe for guidance is as much about the realignment of your inner world as it is about manifesting your outer world. Your intuition and vibrational feedback will likely ask you to do one of these four things: clear, heal, restore (all inner work) and manifest (creating in your outer world). No amount of manifesting mojo will magically materialise your desires if you haven't cleared the way for them first.

The Universe Talks, the Heart Listens (and Talks Back)

Following your heart is about so much more than you may have realised. The heart is an intermediary between you and the wider world, an antenna of sorts, transmitting your desires to the Universe and receiving guidance on how to make them happen. Activate that antenna and get ready to receive and transmit information with the Universe. Your heart asks for what you want and allows the Universe to *show* you how to get it. The feedback through your heart will focus you on the clearing, healing and restoring so you can adjust your energy, because the Universe is all about the vibe. Change yours, and you can attract what you want, or repel what you don't. To follow your heart, then, you need to know where it's asking you to go, and it clearly doesn't ask like your mind does.

I mentioned this earlier, but it bears repeating here: **this Universal feedback loop *is* the guidance; your heart continually processes it, fine-tuning its desires and your internal state, resulting in manifestation or feedback for further fine-tuning.**

Manifesting isn't as simple as 'good vibes only' or 'positive thinking'. If only we could write that million dollar cheque and have it magically arrive in our bank accounts! No, manifesting our heart's best life requires a confluence of all the Universal Laws *and an alignment with what's in our hearts*. **No amount of willpower will manifest what's not true to our heart.**

The heart, then, is the missing piece in the manifestation conversation. The heart bridges the gap between intuition and manifestation. It's the interface between the physical and metaphysical worlds, transferring information through frequencies.

In this way, the heart performs three vital roles:

1. It's the true self's spiritual home, our intuitive centre, helping us navigate by feel.

2. It's a Universal antenna, receiving vibrations and the Universe's messages.

3. It's a vibrational transmitter, radiating the frequency of our desires out into the world.

Is Your Heart Willing?

Time to ask your heart if it's *willing* to work with this process, to build a simple daily ritual to access your intuition and manifest your best life. Put your left hand on your heart, take a deep breath and feel what is in your heart. Nervousness? Excitement? Apprehension? Anticipation? Good! You're ready (and even if you're not, your heart has led you this far, so let's see where else it wants to lead you – the Law of Compensation will reward you).

Take another deep breath, bring all your awareness to your heart again and repeat the question. Go a little deeper, noticing how it *feels*, the sensations in your body, any perceived positive or negative responses, any emotions that arise and how your mind may want to interfere. Do your head and heart answer differently? Note everything in your journal, along with any ideas about what these sensations may mean (you'll learn to interpret them later).

Congratulations! You've just listened to your heart, perhaps for the very first time. Your *willingness* to courageously follow your heart will ignite great change in your life. Now, let's take that vibration of willingness and create a highly personalised ritual of listening to and following your heart.

Recap

- ♥ All of life supports you and is governed by Universal Laws.

- ♥ The Universe responds to your vibration, regardless of what the vibration is.

- ♥ Receiving guidance and manifesting desires are both possible because of Universal Laws. They use the same process.

- ♥ The heart is an antenna, simultaneously transmitting and receiving vibrational information to and from the Universe. The heart is the vital link between intuition and manifesting and the central hub of the feedback loop.

- ♥ This Universal feedback loop *is* the guidance. The heart continually processes the feedback, fine-tuning its desires and internal state, to manifest in physical form.

- ♥ Feedback points you inward (to clear, heal or restore) before pointing you outward to manifest and create in your life. This is the Guidance Cycle.

- ♥ Your *willingness* to develop a daily ritual to tune into your heart and manifest its desire is your new intention and it has begun a vibrational chain reaction. Now, we harness it.

CHAPTER TWO

MIXED MESSAGES

If the heart is an antenna, the head – the rational, logical mind – is a scrambler, creating interference in the signals the heart receives and transmits. Such scrambling makes the signal unintelligible or difficult to detect, resulting in a sound akin to the static when a radio isn't quite tuned to the station: the message can sort of be made out, but there's a lot of irritating noise in the way. The heart's desires can be scrambled by the mixed messages of the head, compounded by responsibilities, others' expectations and the roles we (knowingly and unknowingly) have to fulfil.

Logic rules supreme in the modern, Western world. Override your feelings, bottle up your emotions and push through your body's symptoms. Placing production and achievement on a pedestal, you'd better maintain a constant trajectory of growth to fulfil those ambitious, productive goals – or die trying. An array of rules, roles and expectations are collected from our family of origin, the broader society and culture. Without review, many of these rules, roles and expectations may further scramble the Universal signals received and transmitted by your heart, blinding you to the subtle Universal language that is your birthright.

To follow your heart, you must first clear the clutter and unscramble the interference. In this chapter, you'll identify how your mind muffles and mutes your heart. You'll peel back the layers of beliefs, expectations and conditioning your head holds you hostage to. Unscrambling these thoughts, and their frequencies, gives you the opportunity to choose to continue operating according to them or not (and yes, some of them are useful and even if they're not, we may not be quite ready to let them go).

Unscrambling and decoding the messages your heart receives requires tapping into your intuition. The heart communicates via intuition just as much as it transmits the guidance of the Universal feedback loop. Intuition provides the Inspired Action required in accordance with Universal Law. As you spiral deeper and deeper into that feedback loop, more and more Inspired Action is intuitively acquired thanks to a simple four-step process I call the ARIA Method. That's a neat little acronym for Asking for, Receiving, Interpreting and Acting on your guidance – whether that's your intuition or Universal guidance. The ARIA Method underpins your daily rituals for accessing your intuition, following your heart and manifesting your best life. Start by relinquishing the head's control and opening to the world of information just below the surface.

Head versus Heart

The Law of Polarity reminds us we need both the head and the heart, balancing the two, rather than one dominating the other. But the head won't go down without a fight! It's meant to keep you safe; it wants to protect you from any number of perceived dangers, even if that danger in modern times is less about outwitting animal predators. You might like to think about it this way:

HEART	HEAD
Love	Fear
Intuition	Logic
Flowing	Planning
Open-hearted	Narrow-minded
Non-judgemental	Judgemental
Life force, Universal energy	Mental energy
Rhythmic and cyclical	Linear
Flexible	Fixed
Infinite possibilities	Limited options
Forward-looking	History focused

Default programming has the mind running the show, contributing more fear and worry, a reliance on logic over feeling, and a focus on productivity and output. Your Inner Critic may reside here, too, hurling constant criticism and critiquing your every move, thought and decision. The head scrambles the heart's messages, which is a shame, as the mind's viewpoint tends to be rather limited; it doesn't know *all* the answers. The heart, however, can attune to infinite Universal wisdom.

Both the head and the heart are needed, but if the head has been running things by default, it's time for it to step aside and let the heart be heard. The Head versus Heart exercise at the end of the chapter will help you with this.

Follow Your Heart – Not Someone Else's

Tasked with keeping you safe, the head formulates, then relies upon, an internalised set of rules – typically absorbed as a child from your family of origin, your culture or society – and rarely updates the programming. Consciously questioning and releasing any preconceived limits you (or others) have imposed opens the way for your heart to have a say.

ROLE DESCRIPTIONS

Consider all the roles you play in your life – mother, daughter, employee, friend – and the expectations that go along with those roles. List them in your journal, noting both the explicit and the implicit expectations. Are there key tasks? Are there Key Performance Indicators? If this was a job, what would the pay-off or remuneration be? What hours are you required to be available and how much time, or energy, does this role take up? Once you've exhausted your list, review the roles and 'job descriptions' you've written. Ask yourself:

- ♥ Does this role and/or its expectations reflect who I really am, or am I fulfilling someone else's expectations of me?

- ♥ Does this role and the associated expectations reflect what's in my heart?

- ♥ Where does this role and its expectations really come from? Whose path is it, really?

> ♥ What if I changed the role and job description? (You might even like to rewrite them.)

Blindly following such roles and expectations without review and questioning comes at the expense of following your heart. Unfortunately, our significant others may derail us from following our true heart's desires (even if unintentionally) as they try to guide and steer us. But it's not just those closest to us. Everyday interactions are laced with others' fears, insecurities, judgements and agendas (especially if it requires handing over money). Think about these common interactions, some of which you've likely already had today:

♥ What are today's news headlines? What is real news and what is fearmongering and clickbait? Do you want to align with that energy?

♥ Scrolling social media, how many posts tried to convince you your life needs improving? Did they appeal to your heart, or your head?

♥ What led you into your current career or job? Whose idea was it? Was your choice based on others' advice or experiences, or their hopes or fears for you? Was there something else you really wanted to do?

♥ Are you influenced by the current 'dating rules' or 'relationship goals' society subscribes to? Are these rules real? Do they mirror what's true to your heart?

Don't get side-tracked by others' ideas for you. *Follow what's true for you. Navigate by heart.*

Intuit the Vibe

Intuition converts the vibrational signals from the Universe, as received by our hearts, into data our heads can use. Intuition is an illogical, intangible *feeling* suggesting it's time to act, to move in a particular direction or to take Inspired Action. Notice the emphasis on *feeling*? Sounds an awful lot like how we explained our hearts, right? Each vibration is *felt* in our body, as a hunch, an ailment, a symptom. With practice, we can interpret these messages via our inner wisdom.

Although intuition is largely an internal navigation system, external signs or signposts will pop up from time to time, guiding you further. Unfortunately, these signs are rarely neon flashing lights; they're typically far more subtle, requiring patience and practice to notice and interpret (you will learn more about it in the coming chapters). For now, slow down and observe the synchronicities, 'coincidences' or 'strange' occurrences as much as you notice your feelings and hunches. The intention of willingness has been set; the Universe is already responding. You're about to see how your intuition already knows what all this vibrational and symbolic data means.

The ARIA Method

The Universe talks, the heart listens and answers back – *but how*? Unlike our conversations' reliance on verbal and non-verbal communication, the Universe is less interested in the language and more focused on the *vibrations* of that communication. **To manifest answers and opportunities, we communicate via energy, intentions and our heart's vibration.** We receive the answers and opportunities vibrationally first, then use our intuition to decipher and interpret all of this into Inspired Action steps to take the vibration into physical form.

This can happen almost simultaneously, sometimes it takes longer. Either way, it happens via the ARIA Method, which requires us to develop a *relationship* with our guidance and the Universe just like any other relationship where we expect to give and receive. It's a two-way feedback loop, not a one-way conversation. Please don't be that friend.

Each of the following four chapters dives deeper into the ARIA Method, but to summarise it here:

1. *Asking* focuses our energy, intention and awareness on what we want to attract to ourselves, whether it be guidance, solutions or manifesting our dreams. Vibration is key.

2. *Receiving* requires an openness to, and observation and awareness of, the myriad ways the Universe responds, including through the heart, signs and symbols.

3. *Interpreting* requires familiarity with the symbolic and vibrational language of the Universe, deciphered via intuition for our heads to work with.

4. *Acting* on that guidance is required, not only because it's Universal Law (the Law of Inspired Action) but because without the action we won't be able to fulfil our role. We must be able to determine when and how we act on the guidance given to continue the feedback loop, so the Universe can reward us.

When it feels like your intuition isn't working, or you're struggling to manifest, review the ARIA Method. Chances are one of these four areas is letting you down (not your intuition or manifesting prowess).

The Guidance Practice

Your heart is now primed and ready to lead the show, but its approach will be different. Using the ARIA Method, you'll engage with yourself and your life in a whole new way. Working with the ARIA Method as part of a daily guidance practice, you'll engage with the Universe, refining your vibration to ask for (and receive) what you really want, with your intuition – that inner knowing of your heart – helping you turn all that *feeling* back into useful, logical information for the head to run with.

Your practice will expand exercise by exercise, moving through the remainder of the book, building your intuitive muscle, developing 'proof' of the process to appease your mind before tasking it with the Inspired Actions required. As you add a technique or tool to your repertoire, work with it daily. By the end of the book, you'll have a very personalised ritual. While I don't encourage skipping ahead on your first read through the book, Chapter Eleven may be useful if at any point you're unsure of your daily ritual. Preferably, you'll trust your own heart for now, rather than peek ahead.

For this daily practice, you'll need:

- ♥ a journal, which you should already have a few notes in, and something to write with

- ♥ oracle cards or similar (explored in Chapter Eight)

- ♥ earphones/device if you wish to include guided meditation or music

- ♥ somewhere comfy to sit or meditate.

A dedicated space in your home, just for you, to practise your ritual uninterrupted, is ideal. For me, this is my favourite seat in my bedroom, overlooking the trees, with a special table storing my journal, oracle cards and a few books. If such a space is available to you, set it up with things you love – perhaps flowers, crystals, candles, a special tea set – ready to go each day. If such a space isn't possible, a beautiful basket or bag can work just as well, transporting it as needed each day. Ultimately, the practice is more important than the space.

Is It the Head or the Heart?

Below is an exercise to help you distinguish your head from your heart.

HEAD VERSUS HEART

Select something in your life you're currently pondering, like a change in job, your health or the state of your important relationships. Write this down in your journal, across the top of a blank page. Underneath what you've just written, create a table filling the remainder of the page, with the following headings:

HEAD	HEART
HOW IT FEELS TO THINK	HOW IT FEELS TO BE

Now, take a deep breath to centre yourself. Sit quietly and *think* about this question or situation. Allow your head to come up with every thought possible, writing everything your head offers you in the 'Head' quadrant (top left).

While thinking about this problem, pay attention to how it feels in your body. What does your head/mind feel like while thinking? What physical sensations come up in your body when you think about this problem? Write them down in the 'How it feels to think' box you've drawn (bottom left).

Once you've exhausted all the thinking, take a deep breath and let go of everything that just came up. You may want to stretch before centring yourself again.

Repeat this process, but this time approach the question from your heart. Drop your awareness into your heart centre. Open yourself up in this expansive, loving, non-judgemental place. You may like to meditate or focus on your breathing as you bring your question or problem back to your awareness. Allow yourself to *feel* a response. You might observe emotions, physical sensations – just record whatever comes up in the 'heart' column (top right). How does it feel in your heart? Record this in the 'How it feels to be' box (bottom right).

You should now have a clear indicator of how both the head and heart approach the same situation, and an awareness of how your body responds to each. You've just commenced your daily ritual! Connect with both your head and heart each morning, deepening your skill. Try asking both your head and heart what they need to focus on today, paying attention if you notice the same sensations during the remainder of your day. Record everything in your journal. You'll expand on this in the coming chapters.

Recap

- ♥ Both your head and heart have a role to play, although they have competing agendas.

- ♥ Redefining the head's rules, roles and expectations allows your heart to be heard.

- ♥ Intuition translates the vibrational symbolic language received and transmitted through the heart into more logical action steps.

- ♥ Communication with the Universe has four aspects (the ARIA Method):
    - **Asking** for what you want
    - **Receiving** from the Universe
    - **Interpreting** and translating the communication via intuition
    - **Acting** on the inspired guidance.

- ♥ This ongoing process can be enhanced with a few small steps every day (the Guidance Practice).

- ♥ Your daily ritual now focuses on the Head versus Heart exercise each morning.

CHAPTER THREE

ASKING

I'll hazard a guess there's at least one big question swirling around in your mind right now. Maybe your Big Swirling Question, or BSQ, is about your life's direction and purpose, or a major life choice is keeping you up at night. Maybe you long for the next big love (or money, or children, or opportunity) to arrive. Such questions occupy the mind and can scramble what the heart transmits and receives – but, if allowed to get to work, the heart can help answer the very question that preoccupies the mind. To follow our heart, we must be clear and intentional about what we want to co-create with the Universe, ensuring it is indeed from our heart and not just our head. Such clarity of intention is more crucial to the asking than the mind may have given it credit for.

Perhaps without even realising, you've *always* been asking the Universe for what you want. Universal Laws work with or without your awareness of them. A lack of awareness may have left the mind to run wild, leading to mixed results. Equally, a lack of clarity on what you want will also have led to mixed results. Now, with a greater awareness of how these laws work, you'll harness them, dramatically changing your results by asking from your heart, which is not the kind of asking the mind is currently familiar with. We need to ask the Universe a little differently (hint: it's all about the vibe).

In this chapter, we'll explore the different ways we ask the Universe for what we want (and how our results may change depending on which one we use). We'll look at:

1. **The Big Swirling Questions, or BSQs** – the big, often all-consuming, questions about life direction, purpose and/or major life decisions.

2. **Our heart's core desire** – since it is dormant underneath the surface, we must look a little deeper (and, spoiler alert, the BSQ is pointing towards it) to *feel* the heart's desire.

3. **Supporting questions** – like a romcom leading lady's affable best friend, these questions support the BSQ, but don't steal its spotlight.

Understanding these three ways of asking, you can clarify what you're asking for, how you're asking for it and how you'll make it happen. But you don't do it alone – you'll co-create it with the Universe.

How the Head Asks: Your BSQ

Take a moment to really *think* about your BSQ and, using the following prompts, record your answers in your journal:

- ♥ What is your current BSQ?

- ♥ How much mental energy does it take up?

- ♥ How long have you been thinking about/asking this question?

- ♥ Is there a theme or pattern to your BSQs over time?

- When thinking of your BSQ, what kind of energy or emotion do you feel? Where do you feel that energy or emotion in your body?

- How positively framed is your BSQ?

- How often do you discuss this question/topic with others? Who do you discuss it with?

- Have you received any answers to this question to date?

Talking about your BSQ ad nauseum, constantly pondering it and pleading for insight, generates a frequency you probably don't really want the Universe to match. The Universe doesn't listen to your words (nor the nuance, semantics or implied messages); it is attuned to your feelings, or, more accurately, the *vibration* of those feelings. The Laws of Vibration, Attraction and Correspondence remind us that everything is vibrating, including our thoughts, intentions and actions. Their frequency is what attracts or repels your answers or solutions, not the words or semantics of your language.

Chances are those BSQs are causing you some angst right now, some sort of confusion and challenge – so guess what kind of frequency they hold and what the Universe might return to you? Ruminating on your BSQ often leads to more mental exertion and exhaustion – not a frequency you would want the Universe to match, right? The Universe will respond to the dominant vibration, the frequency you hold most often (think of it as a vibrational base level). **The Universe matches**

your vibrational base level because that's the frequency at which you most often vibrate. Small changes in your base level won't matter too much, but over time, bringing your base level to a higher vibration will attract more of what your heart aligns with. We'll return to the idea of changing the base level shortly.

How to Ask Your BSQ

Although the head offers an understanding of the perceived question or problem, **we can't solve the problem with the same *mind* that created it.** Instead, we must become curious about how we can change the vibrational base level. Approaching the problem with our hearts opens a whole new line of questioning.

Viewed through a different lens, BSQs reveal what precludes us from the very frequency we desire, pointing us inward to the thoughts, beliefs, past hurts or emotional wounds we need to address so our frequency can change. Peeling back these inner layers, we arrive at the heart of the question and a new line of questioning arises for the Universe to answer. Logic can help us here (see, it *is* useful!) and help us understand the mind's repetitive questions.

With your journal at the ready, let's revisit your current BSQ:

♥ Write your current BSQ in your journal again.

- ♥ What is this BSQ really about? Allow the question itself to reveal what's underneath the surface. Try journaling your answers to:
  - What am I worried might (or might not) happen?
  - What fears or concerns does this BSQ represent?
  - Whose fear or concern is this really?
  - What would be the worst thing to happen if this situation wasn't improved? What if it was?

- ♥ What does your heart really need, to address this issue?

- ♥ What is the feeling, sensation or frequency of that desire? Perhaps there's a word or phrase that sums it up for you?

Many of my clients have BSQs about their purpose and finding a meaningful career, typically one that fits around family life. So let's see how this example BSQ stacks up when we break it down.

QUESTIONS	ANSWERS
What is my BSQ?	How do I find meaningful work, perhaps run my own business and contribute financially, and still be hands-on with my children?
What is this BSQ really about?	I want to fulfil my potential, as a mother and in my own work. I want my own needs to be met too.
What am I worried might (or might not) happen?	I'll lose myself and my identity. I'll become resentful. I won't fulfil my dreams. My relationship with my family will suffer. That I can't have it all.

QUESTIONS	ANSWERS
Whose fear or concern is this really?	A 'good mum' is always available and gives everything to her kids. My mother gave up everything for us.
Worst thing if this didn't improve?	I wouldn't fulfil my own dreams.
What does my heart need?	My own identity, meaningful work, to express and create in a way that lights me up. To show my children the possibilities.
What word/phrase sums this up?	Freedom to express myself (and my needs).

In this example, we can see the head and heart want two different things, and the BSQ is already hinting at it. Arriving at that core word or phrase, like 'freedom to express myself and my needs', you've landed on your *heart's core desire*. Now use it to change up your manifesting game.

Our goal isn't to remove our BSQs – or even smaller, less swirly questions, for that matter. Instead, harnessing the benefits of our head *and* heart will bring better solutions. The Law of Polarity tells us so.

Asking from the Heart

Your heart's core desire vibrates at a resonance or frequency the Universe can engage with, one that's totally different to the BSQ, therefore attracting different results. When the heart's core desire becomes the vibrational base level – that is, when you focus on it more than the angst of the BSQ – you've given the Universe a new frequency to match. Work with the exercise below to expand upon your heart's core desire – which must align with your intention, energy, beliefs and actions.

ASKING FOR YOUR HEART'S DESIRES

My heart's core desire is

_____

Now, let's align your intentions, energy, beliefs and actions with that desire.

1. INTENTION | What do I intend to co-create with the Universe?
Just by holding the intention to do so, you now intend to create and attract more of this feeling by working with the Universe to bring yourself into alignment with this desire.

2. ENERGY | Does my energy support or block this intention?
Scan your body – is there resistance, mistrust, tension or fear as you hold the intention? Make a note of these. You'll learn to work with them later in the book.

3. BELIEFS | Do my beliefs support co-creating with the Universe, or do they block it?
Notice any thoughts your mind may interject with – are they open and loving, or are they trying to derail this process?
Make a note of these for now. You'll learn how to work with them soon.

4. ACTIONS | Are my actions in alignment with what I intend to co-create, or are they in opposition?
Am I focused on doing the exercises, have I set up my sacred space, am I approaching this with an open heart? Am I following through with the small layers of my daily ritual? If not, what's the resistance really about?

Record your impressions in your journal. Over the coming chapters you'll learn how to work through the realignment process.

The Supporting Questions

Additional questions geared towards your personal growth, inner transformation and realignment process will crop up alongside your BSQ and heart's desire. The head wants to be put to work; it'll ask *how to fulfil the heart's desire.* Supporting questions allow the focus to move from a BSQ into more manageable Inspired Actions for growth and change. These smaller questions generally don't hang around as long as a BSQ and are less likely to be as vibrationally significant. However, they can still be a very useful source for receiving guidance and answers. While there are any number of supporting questions that may arise (and I've included some examples at the end of the chapter) they can all be summarised in this one question:

What do I need to know today for my inner growth, moving me towards my heart's desire?

A few things about this question I want to point out:

- ♥ It's open (meaning it requires more than a yes or no answer, which is a closed question).

- ♥ It's focused on personal growth and inner transformation, supporting realignment of our vibration and inner world.

- ♥ It does not focus on anyone other than yourself, so as not to interfere with anyone else's path.

Come back to this supporting question and consider:

- ♥ What do you notice when you bring this supporting question into your mind?

- ♥ And then into your heart?

- ♥ What kind of energy and emotion does your body respond with?

- ♥ Does this feel different to when you focus your awareness and attention on your BSQ?

Supporting questions may feature more predominantly as you deepen your practice of the ARIA Method through the remainder of the book. For now, it's ok for the BSQ and, more importantly, your heart's core desire, to take the lead.

What Not to Ask

Some questions are best avoided, and I've listed them briefly below. Feel into them and ask your own heart if they are questions you want to pursue:

- ♥ *Questions about the timing of someone's death.* Perhaps this is one of life's mysteries for a reason, and best kept that way. While I won't specifically ask this question, I may receive a broad intuitive sense that it's time to tie up loose ends or come to a place of peace or forgiveness. Often, this is answer enough.

- ♥ *Questions designed to avoid lessons or challenges.* Asking how to get out of trouble, avoid responsibility or shirk karma? Good luck! That kind of energy will catch up with you. The Law of Compensation and the Law of Attraction say so.

- ♥ *Questions about other people's lessons.* Stay in your lane, focused on your path, your life lessons, your own growth. If asking about others, frame your question so it's focused on *your* role in the relationship – what *you're* learning, what *you're* contributing, for example. Lovingly leave their lessons to them.

Where and When to Ask

Vibrations don't have an off switch. Energy is constantly being exchanged with the Universe (the Law of Balance), meaning we are always asking, all of the time. The more we align our heart's core desire to become our vibrational base level, the more opportunity the Universe will have to match it. To achieve this, we begin layering in our daily ritual, bringing our awareness to our hearts as often as possible. Then we actively work to change and improve the default vibration – but more on that in coming chapters.

For at least a few minutes a day, and more over time, bring your awareness to your heart's desire, following the steps in the exercise below. Add this to your daily routine, returning to it at least once a day, more often if possible. Try it while you're waiting in line, at work, out with friends or in any other situation. With practice, and the more you clear, heal and restore your inner layers, this will become your new default vibration.

EXPANDING THE VIBRATION OF YOUR HEART'S DESIRE

♥ Close your eyes and recall your heart's core desire. Fill your heart with that feeling. (You may need to imagine a new future, or remember a time when you felt this before.)

♥ Connect with that feeling. Bring all your attention to it, noticing where the feeling resides in your body. How big is it?

♥ Invite the feeling to grow, making it big enough to fill your entire body. Continue expanding it as far as it can go today – filling the room you're in, the entire building, the street, the suburb, and so on. Over time, this will grow and your starting point and the size of the feeling will change.

- ♥ Observe any other sensations or emotions that are present while you do this, without attaching to them.

- ♥ When you feel ready, thank this frequency and ask it to stay in this expanded state for as long as possible.

- ♥ Gently bring yourself back to the present moment, and open your eyes. Notice how you feel now, with this expanded frequency still present.

- ♥ Set yourself a reminder to check in on this feeling (and how expanded it is) throughout your day. If it has diminished, use this technique to again expand.

Remember to record any observations in your journal each time you do this.

Build Your Ritual

As you're building your daily ritual, remember the three ways of asking:

1. your BSQ

2. your heart's core desire – and expanding it as your dominant frequency

3. your supporting questions.

Returning to your ritual each morning, check these three things by:

- ♥ connecting with the BSQ and the heart's core desire just underneath it

- ♥ spending a few minutes expanding the vibration of your heart's desire

- ♥ using the supporting questions (see sample below) as journaling prompts. If more questions arise during your practice, simply repeat these three steps.

Check in on your heart's core desire throughout your day, too. Record your observations in your journal.

SAMPLE SUPPORTING QUESTIONS

Starter question:
What do I need to know today for my inner growth, moving me towards my heart's desire?

Daily questions:
How does my heart feel today?
What does my heart need today?
What do I need to take care of myself today – physically, mentally, emotionally and spiritually?
Where can I bring myself back into alignment?
What small steps can I take today to bring alignment?

For the Big Swirling Question:
How is this current challenge in my life serving me?
What am I learning?
How can I grow from this situation?

What do I need to let go of, or heal, inside myself to improve this situation?

How can I bring a new perspective to this area of my life?

How is this impacting other areas of my life? How are they connected?

For the inner work:
Who or what am I ready to let go?

What am I healing?

Where do I need to restore?

What does my heart truly want me to create more of in my life? How?

Recap

- ♥ Awareness of your questions and focus is important, but how it *feels* is paramount.

- ♥ Position your curiosity around personal growth and development.

- ♥ Keep the line of questioning open, not closed.

- ♥ The Universe is always listening, but can only 'hear' the vibration of your asking.

- ♥ Continue doing your ritual for a few minutes each day, especially the Expanding the Vibration of Your Heart's Desire exercise and journaling, until you layer in the next chapter's tools.

CHAPTER FOUR

RECEIVING

Have you ever felt a pang in your heart when a gift, or a thoughtful gesture, or even a heartfelt compliment you offered someone wasn't well received? The Law of Balance describes our inherent instinct to give and receive from others in a balanced way, the Universe included. Imagine what message (and vibration) you send when you don't wholeheartedly receive what's on offer – although, we can be *discerning* in our receivership. More on that in a moment.

Maybe you've been on the other side of this – for example, buying and sending gifts out of obligation (Christmas, anyone?). This is a completely different proposition to giving a gift from a place of genuine thought and care – and it can be felt by the recipient. Receiving is not just about the physical receiving, but also the mental, emotional and energetic receiving. Conversations about manifesting so often focus on the *physical manifestation* (say, the *object* of our desires) but we now know it's all about the vibe. **We must receive our manifestations energetically before we receive them physically.**

Receiving pleasure, goodness and abundance is incredibly uncomfortable or unfamiliar for some. Desire alone will not change your ability to welcome in such blessings when they arrive (kind of like how an influx of money can quickly burn a hole in our pockets). Similarly, tolerating an undesirable experience in the name of receiving is not the vibrational sweet spot either. **Receiving is about the *vibration* on offer more than the offer itself.** Recognising and receiving the vibration of the message, we can then interpret and act – and decide if it's something we wish to continue inviting in.

Before we reach the interpreting and acting, our focus here is the receiving phase of the ARIA Method. Observing ourselves and our immediate environment in new ways, we can recognise, and discerningly receive, the abundance of Universal guidance and gifts coming our way. Answers always come – it's Law. But if we don't recognise the guidance and solutions when they arrive, we've missed the opportunity, falsely believing our intuition, or this process, isn't working. It is.

Tune Your Antenna with Gratitude

Knowing your heart is an antenna for receiving the Universe's messages, you may be wondering how you actually tune the antenna to receive. Cultivate a state of receiving through practising gratitude. One of the quickest ways to recognise your ability to receive is to gratefully recognise what you have already received. The Universe doesn't discern if your vibration is associated with something physically, tangibly happening right now, or if it is attached to an imagined or daydreamt state; it just recognises the vibration. Practising the vibration of receiving, or gratitude, can trigger an influx of more (even if your current reality feels less than abundant).

Feeling grateful when stuck in a relationship rut, or challenged by change, is indeed tricky, but by reframing our thoughts we reframe our vibration (and therefore, what we will receive). Undeniably, certain privileges exist (that must be recognised in order to be grateful for them), just as certain disadvantages exist. Gratitude isn't about glossing over such gross inequalities or inequities. However, if we can task ourselves with finding people and things to be grateful for, we can shift our vibrational experience, if not yet our physical one. Focusing on what we don't have invites a vibrational match to that sense of perceived lack. If we focus on being grateful for what we do have, then we're vibrationally asking to receive more to be grateful for.

Positivity cannot bypass negativity. In fact, the brain is wired in such a way that it is constantly scanning for the negative, in what psychologists call 'the negativity bias'. We may not be able to override this (and the Law of Polarity suggests we need both positivity *and* negativity, anyway), but we can learn to counter it by actively and consciously scouting for the positive *as well*. Gratitude is not about ignoring what needs attention. Instead, it is an opportunity to recognise our current Universal gifts, thus shifting our vibration back to our heart's truth and activating our antenna for more. From there, we can influence the change we wish to see.

Let's practise an attitude of gratitude with the following exercise.

PRACTISING GRATITUDE

1. Grab your journal and pen and write down five people or things you are grateful for.

2. Review the list, *feeling* that gratitude in your heart as you connect with each person or thing on your list. Can you expand its presence?

3. Now write down another five people or things and repeat the process.

4. Continue until you have exhausted the process for today.

Add this gratitude practice to your growing daily ritual – but there is one small caveat: you cannot repeat an inclusion. Each day, be on the lookout for new things, experiences, places and people to express your gratitude for (and double points if you recognise how you and the Universe co-created this!). This is a particularly nice exercise to do at the close of each day.

Combining Multiple Antennas: The Four Bodies

I'm starting to regret the antenna metaphor, because I just had to research how you can combine multiple antennas to receive different channels, as a way of explaining this next concept. But, bear with me … A combiner allows multiple antennas to merge their signals into a single stream of information, or to receive multiple channels, like on your television. Enter the multiple antennas: your Four Bodies – the physical, mental, emotional and energetic layers – which can combine to allow multiple additional messages to be received.

Just like your thoughts have their own vibrations, so too do the other layers of your being, according to the Law of Vibration, which says *everything* is made up of energy. Your beliefs, behaviours and emotions all have their own vibration, contributing to your overall personal vibrational set point. Meanwhile, the Law of Correspondence explains that what happens in one of these Four Bodies will influence the others, giving rise to corresponding signs and symptoms. Adding in the Laws of Cause and Effect and Perpetual Transmutation of Energy, we can observe that symptoms, ailments, complaints, concerns or blocks in any one of these Four Bodies can provide answers, as well as healing and change, to the other bodies. No matter whether we start with improving our physical, mental, emotional or energetic bodies, there will be a knock-on effect on the other layers. Everything is connected, as the Law of Divine Oneness says.

Our thoughts, beliefs and experiences, together with our emotions, wounds and hurts, all have their own vibration, and those vibrations can be stored in our bodies, and in our energy field or energetic body. When those vibrations interfere with, or alter, our personal vibrational base level, we vibrate at a lower frequency than we are designed to. The Universe won't consider the nuance or give us a free pass; it will just respond to the vibration it finds. Thankfully, the feedback loop shows us where such lower-vibing thoughts, beliefs, behaviours and emotions are creating that vibrational misalignment. Then we can work to change them, bringing our vibrational set point higher again.

WHAT ARE THE FOUR BODIES?

Physical: most specifically this covers our anatomical body, but more broadly it can include possessions (including money), people and places.

Mental: thoughts, thinking, beliefs, perceptions, stories and assigned meanings.

Emotional: the range of emotions we feel (or avoid).

Energetic (or spiritual): the vibrations and frequencies in our energy field as well as the flow of Universal life force energy through those energy systems.

Your Four Bodies' Signals

Whether you've been aware of it or not, each of these Four Bodies has been communicating with you your whole life. Let me give you some examples:

- ♥ Have you ever been in love? How did you know?

- ♥ Have the hairs on the back of your neck or on your arms ever stood to attention?

♥ Ever had butterflies in your tummy?

♥ Have you ever felt 'sick to your stomach' about something? Described someone as 'a real pain in the neck'? Felt 'stuck in a rut'? Maybe you've 'welled up' or had a 'lump in your throat'?

♥ Have you ever used a particular phrase, or explained a situation in a certain way, that caught your attention, because you were surprised to hear that's what you really thought?

♥ Has your body ever expressed an undercurrent of sensation you couldn't quite figure out – maybe depression or anxiety, even an excited anticipation – without an obvious, logical reason why?

♥ Have you ever thought your life probably appears great from the outside looking in, but from your perspective, not so much (without being able to put your finger on why)?

If you answered yes to any of these, then you, my friend, have had your Four Bodies talking to you. Even if you answered no to all the questions, it doesn't mean they aren't trying to reach you. Their communication may be very obvious (as in the first few examples) or far more subtle clues (like the last few dot points).

The following exercise will help you identify the messages from these combined antennas – or, more accurately, how you receive the messages through each antenna individually.

The exercise should only take a few minutes and can be added to your daily ritual. With repeated practice, you'll be far more attuned to your body's wisdom, not just your heart's. When combined, you'll have streams and streams of vibrational data to interpret and act on. Thank you, antenna combiner!

WHAT YOUR FOUR BODIES TELL YOU

Take a deep breath, filling your belly, then your chest. Pause. Then exhale, emptying your chest, then your belly. Do this a few times to centre yourself in your body.

You may like to close your eyes, then scan your body from top to toe, noting anything you observe in your body as you scan:

- ♥ What sensations do you notice in your body?

- ♥ How much energy do you have?

- ♥ What emotions arise? Where?

- ♥ What does your body need more of right now?

- ♥ What does your body need less of?

- ♥ What does your mind do in response to these observations?

Record your observations in your journal. Also record any insights you have about what these impressions mean (we'll learn more about that shortly).

The Four Bodies reveal what is ailing or failing us, bringing lower vibrations to the surface to be recognised. We don't want to hang out in that lower vibration too long. Instead, we can use gratitude as a quick way to raise our vibration in the short term, while also working in the longer term to realign our internal state. For now, note these lower-vibrational areas in your journal. We'll start to clear, heal and restore them soon.

Beyond the Antennas: Signs, Symbols and Messengers

The Universe gets your attention via other means if the antenna's messages aren't being received (which, by the way, will have more to do with the antenna than the signal itself). When viewed with a new lens, your external world – your complex web of real-life people, relationships, jobs and experiences happening right now – can offer additional vibrational clues via the feedback loop. And the Universe will throw in some serendipitous signs, symbols and messengers for good measure. There's a world of symbolic, intuitive data beyond your heart that your intuition can still receive and translate.

A House of Mirrors

The Law of Correspondence explains that challenges, difficulties or frustrations in our outer world correspond to something being 'off kilter' in our internal world. What we see in the world around us is a reflection of what is inside of us. If we don't like what we see 'out there', we may need to change something 'in here'.

To be clear, we do not cause other people's behaviour (their choices and behaviours are their own). Nor do we need to tolerate intolerable situations. If we are enduring, enabling or excusing an intolerable behaviour or situation, that may be reflecting something inside us that needs to change. Perhaps there is a boundary we need to enforce, or a belief we need to reframe, or some other perception or behaviour we need to change. We cannot change others; we can only change how we perceive and respond. Such mirrors may not reflect an exact image, but instead beam the light inward to illuminate something within you to change (perception, beliefs, behaviours and energy) so that the situation (not necessarily the other person) can change.

The feedback loop provides that mirror, reflecting our inner world in our external world, and vice versa. Working with the ARIA Method and an intention of growth, healing, releasing and change, we can bring ourselves back into alignment internally to make changes externally. These are the Inspired Actions required. Without inner change, any outer world changes – say changing jobs or ending a relationship – will only result in short-term relief before the same vibrational problems arise in the next job, or the next relationship. Things won't change until we do. And the message will repeat until the lesson is learned. Explore this Law of Correspondence via the following Mirror Technique

THE MIRROR TECHNIQUE

In your journal, divide your page into three columns, as in the example below.

SITUATION	REFLECTION	INNER WORK

In the Situation column, make a list of the current situations or relationships that challenge or frustrate you – things you wish to change. Be specific.

In the Reflection column, allow your heart to tell you what this situation may be reflecting to you – an unspoken need? An unkept boundary? A latent desire? A past wound? If you're struggling here, ask yourself this question: 'What do I need to know about this situation for my inner growth?'

In the Inner Work column, record answers to these questions: what needs to be said? What action needs to be made? What support do you need? In the coming chapters, you'll be able to flesh this out more, using your interpreting and acting skills.

Messengers

Many times external answers come through chance meetings, synchronistic conversations or through friends or strangers seemingly randomly answering the BSQ we're pondering. Strangers have approached me with meaningful books. Uber drivers have connected me to important contacts. Clients have unknowingly used phrases and comments I intuited prior to their arrival. While I was contemplating the title of this book, both my daughters and a client used the phrase 'follow your heart' in random conversations. My publisher then suggested it as a title. When the guest judge on *MasterChef* that night told a contestant to follow his heart, I knew we'd landed on the right title.

Not every single encounter is an answer to a question we're pondering. We will recognise when we receive the answer by *how it feels*.

Recognising Signs and Symbols

Just like the message relayed via *MasterChef*, answers and guidance can arrive in other ways than via our internal antennas. The Universe's language is highly symbolic and, if we train our hearts to perceive the magic, we will notice the clues dropped like breadcrumbs. If following the Universe's cryptic crumbs is a new idea for you, come back to at least being *willing* to entertain this idea. Try it out. See what happens.

Recognising these kinds of Universal messages requires us to drop into an observer role, and to view the world with some neutrality (the Law of Relativity) and non-judgement. We cannot orchestrate a sign; we need to allow it (like the way I accepted it randomly appearing on my TV screen in an unlikely show). Observing the world through the lens of your heart, you're more likely to notice the synchronicities, turns of phrase and repetition that turn up.

For some, there are specific signs they recognise. Feathers can symbolise spirit communication. Coins may turn up when working on financial abundance. Butterflies arrive during a change of life phase or stage, while a snake may turn up when you are symbolically shedding a skin (and yes, several uninvited snakes have visited my home). Many people report seeing repeating number patterns (just google 11:11) or repeating phrases or images.

But it's not just feathers, coins, butterflies and the like – anything can make a sign if it hits the right note or frequency. I get an extra kick out of spotting signs in unusual places – like the time I travelled interstate to host an event and the hotel booked for me featured lobby chairs covered in a feather pattern. Or the time I saw '55' carved into a tree in the middle of bushland (it signified change and arrived as I traded my PR job for working as a psychic).

Caution: not everything is a sign. Stay objective and non-attached (the Law of Relativity). The best signs I receive come in unusual, uncanny ways I truly couldn't have orchestrated myself. I've shared many of these in my previous books, podcast episodes and on social media – my favourites have included the radio playing songs sent to me by my deceased loved ones; library books picked up at random only to have the previous reader's printed quote bookmark fall to my feet, containing the answer to my BSQ; and the licence plate on the car that pulled up beside me on my way home from pitching my second book that said 'WRITE'. But the snakes I can live without!

Now, before you say that receiving such a sign is simply a manifestation of your desire for one (which, by the way, makes me happy that you're implementing Universal Laws), let's put this to the test. I didn't ask for a particular song to play on the radio (and even if I did, I'm not *that* powerful to have it air the moment I turned on my car!). I had no knowledge such a licence plate existed, let alone that its owner was also driving home through peak hour traffic on a route I don't normally take. The *MasterChef* guest judge certainly isn't known for his philosophical nature. My perpetual intention is to remain open to receiving and recognising signs, not determining what they should or shouldn't be. That's the Universe's job. Instead, we focus on asking and receiving. Besides, if we could be so intentional with the object of our manifestation, we would all indeed be billionaires.

Asking for a Sign

A client recently combined asking for a sign with her powers of manifestation. She wanted to manifest an invitation, and within a short time an invitation to a party arrived. While at the party, she received an invitation from a colleague in attendance to connect on a business opportunity. By the end of the party, my client felt she was about to receive an invitation on a date – but consciously closed her energy to avoid having to physically turn down the potential suitor.

Now it's your turn to manifest a sign. Use the exercise below, perhaps to manifest your own invitation or to stay open to a solution or answer arriving in relation to your BSQ or a supporting question. This method works for both.

ASKING FOR A SIGN

1. Reconnect with your heart's core desire, or the frequency of the question you'd like answered. Expand that feeling through your body.

2. Make a request to the Universe – in this instance, ask for a sign or messenger to arrive to answer your question.

3. Ensure you feel open and willing to recognise the sign, perhaps having the intention to physically feel the sign when it arrives.

4. With the intention in place, go about your day but be open to an answer turning up.

5. When you notice your sign, thank the Universe (and be sure to include it in tonight's gratitude list).

Record the experience in your journal, along with any impressions regarding what it meant. You'll learn to interpret it shortly.

I'm Not Receiving Anything!

We can't control the timing of our answers or how they turn up – that's up to the Law of Rhythm – but we do need to trust the process. Perhaps the perceived lack of receiving *is* the message – and it's guiding us to address the perception, not the receiving. The feedback loop and energy exchange still occurs, the Universe still provides guidance and data, even if it looks and feels different to your mind's expectations. Repeat the Mirror Technique to unearth any latent beliefs or past wounds that may be preventing or limiting your receiving, whether from the Universe or from others.

As you begin exploring your inner world in relation to your ability to receive, consider these supporting questions (perfect for journaling now, or you can return to them later, with the tools from Chapters Eight, Nine and Ten):

- ♥ As a child, who modelled how to gratefully receive? How did your mum receive? Your dad?

- ♥ What other messages did you absorb about receiving (anything) while growing up? Do you believe you are allowed to receive in your life?

- ♥ Is there a cap or upper limit on what you can receive?

- ♥ Are certain things easier to receive than others? Why?

- ♥ Do you struggle to receive in particular areas of your life?

- ♥ Who or what have you pushed away? Why?

♥ Observe the small ways you receive each day – a compliment, a freebie, a coin on the ground. What does this tell you about your greater ability to receive?

Formulate additional questions here to examine the thoughts, beliefs and actions you have around giving and receiving. Take this line of supporting questions into your daily practice (we'll build more on this in later chapters). Supporting questions peel back inner layers to clear, heal or restore our inner world, improving what we draw to ourselves (manifest). Maintaining the feedback loop, realigning internally and asking more questions brings us back into alignment. And don't forget to keep tuning and combining your multiple antennas.

Create Space to Receive

Where can you create more moments of stillness, space and silence throughout your day, creating an opportunity to recognise and receive from your heart and the Universe? Below are suggestions for you to intuitively feel into, asking if they're right for you in terms of increasing your ability to receive:

♥ do a digital detox

♥ take a social (or traditional) media hiatus

♥ ditch music/earphones while exercising

♥ no reading or scrolling on your commute

- ♥ stick to mono-tasking, not multitasking

- ♥ allow everyday activities (like showering, brushing your teeth) to be mindful moments

- ♥ a few times a week, take your lunch break at work alone, in nature, without a phone or other diversion

- ♥ extend your daily morning routine.

Many existing activities and fleeting moments have been commandeered by the mind, but can again become the heart's domain, inviting in a rush of intuitive data. Give thanks when it does, and more will arrive. Such pockets of stillness, space and silence help to harmonise the Four Bodies, triggering our gratitude and resetting the vibrational set point.

Recap

- ♥ Discerning receivership is about recognising the vibration of who or what is on offer and choosing if we wish to accept it or not.

- ♥ Receiving guidance and support requires the antenna (and our viewpoint) to notice and allow it.

- ♥ You can quickly tune your heart through gratitude.

- ♥ The information from your Four Bodies can be combined to provide additional information about your frequency.

♥ We can also receive guidance and manifest answers through people, signs, symbols and messengers.

♥ Your morning daily ritual can now expand to include:
  – scanning your Four Bodies
  – the Mirror Technique (as needed)
  – asking for a sign and observing who or what turns up
  – gratitude practice each evening
  – recording all your impressions, signs and symbols in your journal.

CHAPTER FIVE

INTERPRETING

Now that you're gratefully recognising and receiving answers and solutions, you can turn your attention to interpreting what they mean. This phase of the ARIA Method may require the most practice. How we interpret something today may change tomorrow. My message's meaning may be different from yours. But practice, and a hefty dose of trial and error, will assist you in curating a personal reference library of interpretations for your intuitive nudges. Intuition comes to the fore in this stage.

Think of intuition as 'inner-tuition', a guiding, teaching inner voice that can translate the feelings, hunches and symbolism into something more useful for the mind. Your intuition already knows exactly what the vibrations, symbolism and messages mean. By developing your intuition, you increase your ability to convert the deep inner knowing into the tangible, logical knowing the mind has been (not so patiently) waiting for.

Answers always come – but our interpretation can be wrong. To minimise the potential pitfalls, I'll share a range of tools and techniques to interpret the Universal messages and answers in your heart – and what to do if you get it wrong. Through our interpretations (and the subsequent supporting questions this stage will produce) we will add context to the vibrations and signs we've gratefully received, appeasing the mind with something more than an intuitive hunch. The ARIA Method can now prove to the mind that there's far more to the feelings the heart transmits and receives, and that your intuition is its translator.

What the Hell Does That Mean?

So far, we've seen that messages can come via vibrations, feelings, our Four Bodies' clues, messengers, external signs, symbols and the feedback loop. Reams of insight reside inside your journal, and you'll add even more to it in the coming chapters when we explore oracles, meditation and expression. With all this intuitive data at your disposal, how do you know what the hell it all means?

Step one is to check whether the manifested message is literal or symbolic. Symbolism is the Universe's modus operandi, but just to keep you on your toes it will at times present you with literal messages. A literal message, for example, may show up physically as a symptom obviously requiring medical attention. A symbolic physical symptom, though, may not need medical attention and could instead be suggesting that something in one of the other bodies needs addressing. Asking for a sign and then continually getting red lights, as another example, could be interpreted literally as a 'do not proceed' regarding the course of action you're asking about. Such literal signs are rare, so receive them gratefully when they arrive! Most messages are far more likely to be symbolic. The subtle physical symptoms, emotions, vibrations, signs and the like require a few intuitive tools when interpreting their meaning.

Tools for Interpretation

Whether we receive messages through our Four Bodies, through signs and messengers, or even in our dreams, we can use the same techniques to interpret what they mean. Here are a few tools I personally work with to interpret my messages and manifestations. You may need to mix and match the methods to add meaning and context to your interpretations.

The Animal Kingdom

Messages often turn up via the animal kingdom. These messages are often easy to interpret when we consider our shared understandings about animals – things we've been taught about them since we were children, like the story of the tortoise and the hare.

Animal messengers may turn up physically (like the snakes who frequent my home) or as references in images, books, media and the like. If such a messenger turns up, consider its symbolism – but only if it's truly a messenger. Seeing your family pet each day isn't a sign. Neither are the expected animals you see when you visit a zoo. But if you ask for a sign and go about your day only to see a truck drive past with a lion logo emblazoned on its carriage, then a jogger runs past with a lion on their jersey, and then a song roars into your ears à la Katy Perry … that's a sign!

In this instance, consider what the lion represents to you. How does it connect to the question you've been asking? What was your vibrational set point when you saw the truck and the jogger, and heard the song? To get you started, I've included the lion along with some other animals and insects in the table below. Consider each creature and what it represents to you, then compare that to my suggested meaning in the right-hand side of the table.

Lion	Strength, leader, royalty (king of the jungle), Leo star sign
Butterfly	Life cycles, rhythms, change, beginnings, metamorphosis, inside a darkened cocoon
Dolphin	Intelligence, calm, family, protection, pods/community
Dog	Best friend, loyal, unconditional love, puppy dog eyes
Moth	Light, illumination, drawn to truth/light
Turtle	Slow and steady, 'you have time', 'just keep swimming', hermit, tough exterior, hiding inside your shell
Snake	Shedding skin, rebirth, spirituality, healing, fertility

Numbers

Earlier I suggested googling 11:11. That search would have retrieved millions of suggestions about angel numbers, manifesting, numerology and spiritual meanings. 11:11 isn't the only number combination people report seeing – there are as many combinations as there are numbers. It's their repetition, or vibrational impact, that makes them a sign. For repeating number combinations, I recommend Doreen Virtue's *Angel Numbers* book. Google can again be your friend here, but it comes with a caveat: please filter the suggested meanings you find online (or elsewhere, for that matter, including here) through your own heart, and your own personal reference point (we'll cover this later in the chapter). A Google search of the number plus 'angel number' – they're considered to be a sign from our guardian angels – can deliver an interpretation starting point. Whether from angels or the Universe more broadly, there is merit in their message. Even if angel numbers aren't your thing, perhaps numerology is. Certain numbers can hold personal, individualised meanings, too, referring to an important date or anniversary, or just a particular month, or a predicted timeframe.

Colours

Colours may make an appearance in meditation, especially guided meditation (see Chapter Nine), or in our dreams (see Chapter Seven). Perhaps we see repeating colours or are drawn to a specific colour during a particular phase or stage of our life. There are a few different ways I interpret colours.

Firstly, many colours are linked to the energy centres in our body, called chakras. Each energy centre has its own theme, and as we process energy around that theme, this energy centre processes those vibrations. If, by chance, you get a reference to such a colour or energy centre, consider it firstly a sign to deal with the themes and associated energy of that centre. For example, questions about family or financial security or your home would be linked to the base chakra, whose colour is red. I briefly share these energy centres and colours in the following table.

This is not a hard and fast rule, of course. We can also interpret colours based on the personal connotations they have for us. Red can also be associated with feelings of passion or anger, meanings that could be worth leaning into here. A personal affinity with a particular colour will sway its meaning for you, as can cultural, religious or societal associations. Consider the colours in the left-hand side of the table below, and then my suggestions on the right, along with any you might add.

Red	Base chakra (family, safety, belonging) Passion, anger, grounding, earthing
Orange	Sacral chakra (creativity, fertility, intuition, interpersonal relationships) Sunburnt country, Netherlands, citrus, vitality
Yellow	Solar plexus chakra (self-image, inner strength, confidence) Sunny, happy, bright, positive
Green	Heart chakra (give and take, love) Nature, healing, emotions
Blue	Throat chakra (expression, communication, choice) Calm, soothing, ocean, feeling down, 'the blues' in music
Purple	Third eye chakra (clairvoyance, clear-seeing, insight, clarity) My grandma, royalty, magic, Lent
White	Crown chakra (spirituality, religion, connection, oneness) Purity, protection, death

You may have completely different associations with these colours (especially to purple!) which may come from personal experience, or your cultural background. We must rely on our own heart's meaning above anyone else's.

Personal Reference Points

Although I've already hinted at this, I do recommend staying open to any message referencing something you've watched, read or personally experienced, especially if it includes parallel themes or lessons. Memories and personal experiences that pop into your awareness may do so as a way of answering your question. Pay close attention to any sort of sign or message that has a particular meaning for you. When I hear *I'll Be Missing You* by Puff Daddy on the radio, I cry (and readers of *You Already Know* may recognise this as the song that played as I drove to the hospital to farewell my dying grandmother). That song, or any other sign, may mean something else entirely to you – or nothing at all!

Keep your eyes, ears and heart open in conversations, while out interacting with the world, for any seemingly random connections. They can be intuitive clues. Countless times clients will relay something, only to stop and say they don't know why they're telling me … but I do!

Plays on Words

Perhaps it's the writer in me, or the punny home I was raised in, but I love a good play on words. Give me a double entendre any day. Apparently, the Universe loves it too. Throughout the book, I've deliberately used certain phrases or idioms when describing our physical, mental, emotional or energetic quandaries – and for good reason. Words are powerful (they too vibrate) and hold an array of meanings, both personal or shared, literal and symbolic. To demonstrate, I've included another table. Start on the left-hand side, considering what the phrase means for you, and then view my suggested interpretations and add to them with your own meanings.

PHRASE	LITERAL	SYMBOLIC
A pain in the neck	I have a sore neck.	Someone/something is causing me pain or challenge.
I've had a gutful	My stomach is quite literally full.	I have reached my limit with this person/situation. My physical, mental, emotional or energetic system cannot process this.
Seeing red	My eyes are literally tinged with red (perhaps you've looked at the sun too long?).	I cannot see clearly because I'm angry about this situation/with this person.
Stuck in a rut	I have literally become stuck in a furrow I cannot get out of.	I'm bored by the established routine or pattern.
Follow your heart	Your heart exists outside your body and is pointing to a pathway.	Your heart is an intuitive antenna and knows where you're going.

Multiple and Hidden Meanings

Such wordplay helps us to see that there can be multiple and hidden meanings inside our messages. For example, when I first developed The Little Sage Oracle Cards, I included a card called 'Inner Child', a reference to the younger, innocent version of you who may need attention or healing (another great source of insight, by the way). Once the cards were in use, I quickly realised that play on words also literally referenced pregnancy.

This also highlights how easy it is for interpretations to change from day to day (today purple is a message from Grandma, tomorrow it's about clairvoyance), or that two people could interpret the same thing entirely differently (purple probably means something other than a sign from my grandma to you, but if it's her, please say hi). Signs require fresh interpretation each time they arrive, no matter how frequently we receive them. Each time, we need to look for additional hidden meanings and personal references, and how these might relate back to our intention, vibration or question.

Patterns and Repetition

Seeing something once may not necessarily make it a sign – but see the same thing in different places, and you may be onto something. You'll often know a sign by how it *feels*. Signs hit a little differently; they'll make you sit up and pay attention and are often hard to forget. But if you miss it, another will come. The Law of Rhythm says so. Next time, it may arrive in a different way, or through a different medium. Hold the intention to receive, and it will always come. Universal whispers can and will eventually become loud clangs about the head if they need to. If you're not sure you've received a sign, ask for another. Then go back to observing, witnessing and recording everything. And if you hear, see or sense the same thing time and time again, it's most likely a sign.

What Do You Make of This?

While I was writing this chapter, a friend asked me for help clarifying a sign she'd received, and I share it below as a great example of going a little deeper into the meaning of a sign *for you*. Play along, using your new intuitive interpretation skills, and see what you make of it.

My friend, an accomplished and successful business owner, was considering whether to expand or simplify her business, so she asked for a sign while out driving. Before long, a truck appeared on the highway beside her carrying what she said were the largest tyres she'd ever seen. Catching herself thinking about how big the truck and tyres were, she realised it was her sign. So far, she'd asked and received. But she didn't know how to interpret the sign.

She sent me a voice message asking me for my take on it. Because my personal interpretation would mean diddly-squat, I asked a few supporting questions ('How did you feel about this truck?' and 'What did the truck or tyres do next?') so we could reveal what this truck and its oversized tyres meant *for her*.

My friend had felt annoyed – she really thought she was going to simplify, and she felt disappointed that the Universe might want her to expand. She also explained that the truck kept encroaching on her lane, keeping her stuck behind it for a while, frustrated that it was slowing her down and she couldn't get around it.

Applying what you've learned so far, what do you think the interpretation here is? At first glance the supersized tyres might hint at expansion, but with some additional interpretation, a completely different meaning is revealed. Here are a few key things I drew her attention to:

- ♥ Her body was frustrated and disappointed – she did not want to expand, she wanted to simplify. Her Four Bodies didn't feel aligned with expanding.

- ♥ Symbolically, the truck and tyres were 'encroaching into her lane'. Expansion wasn't part of her pathway; her lane wasn't about expansion.

- ♥ The oversized truck kept her 'stuck' and 'slowed her progress'. Without the idea of expansion in her way, she could move forward again.

She's now working on simplifying her business. The oversized tyres themselves weren't the answer, but her feelings about them and her perceptions about what was happening were. Your Universal messages may require this distinction, too.

Circling Back to the Feedback Loop

How would you rate your life right now? How does it feel? Does everything flow with ease, or does it feel a bit choppy? Whatever's happening in your outer world, it's feeding back information about what to address in your inner world for realignment. You now have the tools to revisit some of the work you've done to date and begin interpreting these messages:

- ❤ Revisit your answers to the Mirror Technique (Chapter Four) and use the interpretation techniques we just explored, considering the language, colours, patterns and messages. What do they mean?

- ❤ Revisit your Four Bodies exercise (Chapter Four). Look at your notes. How do you now interpret it? What might need course correcting?

- ❤ What signs, symbols and messengers have you received? What do they mean?

Continue interpreting all the messages and impressions in your journal so far. You may identify Inspired Actions – but hold tight for now! Make a note of them and we'll revisit them in the next chapter.

It's Still Unclear!

Supporting questions: take your cue on centre stage. Work with supporting questions now to determine the meanings of your messages, just as I did for my friend and the tyres. Supporting questions can clarify what a feeling, sensation or sign means, through asking for more information. Simply rinse and repeat the ARIA Method.

When I struggle to understand my messages, I may call on additional tools (which we will explore in Part Two) or revisit my heart's core desire or my BSQ. Chances are there's something 'off' internally to address. This gives us an opportunity to layer messages and interpretations, shifting us from a half-hearted hunch to a full-blown knowing. Layers of meaning add contextual data, something our heads will love! Your daily ritual and regular observations are layering multiple data points, which you'll add to in the coming chapters.

Other times, we just need to be patient. The mind assumes all understanding must be at the mental level; that we should cognitively understand what all the messages and manifestations mean. However, our Four Bodies (especially the energetic body) may know before our head does. By working with the feelings in our bodies, and the power of our heart, we will always know the answer, even if our head is unclear.

Putting all these layers of meaning together gives a much clearer picture of your guidance, in a way your mind may appreciate. With all this information, we can move into the final phase of the ARIA Method: acting.

Interpreting Your Signs

The exercise below is the technique to try when reviewing your messages to date, or any new messages from here on in.

INTERPRETING YOUR SIGNS

♥ Notice a sign, symbol or pattern.

♥ Take a deep breath, filling your belly, then your chest.

♥ Pause, then exhale, emptying your chest, then your belly.

♥ Fill yourself with gratitude for the sign.

♥ Consider whether the message is literal or symbolic.

♥ Work with supporting questions to ask: 'What does this sign mean?' or 'What do I need to know about (insert sign or message here)?'

♥ Notice any impressions or sensations that arise in your body or in your heart.

♥ You might also notice your mind's opposition. Allow it to be there, and just notice it.

♥ Review the tools in this chapter and apply the relevant ones.

Try this and then record your impressions, along with the sign, in your journal.

Create a Reference Book

Now, with all these symbols and meanings, you can create a highly personalised index of interpretations. Grab an old-school index book (like an address book, with sections for each letter of the alphabet). Flip to the corresponding letter and add the symbol and your interpretation/s beside it. Start by adding the meanings suggested throughout this chapter. Keep adding to this each time you find a new sign or symbol, or add new meanings to existing signs or symbols.

Additional Interpretation Tools

To add to Google and Doreen Virtue's *Angel Numbers*, here are some further suggested tools:

- ♥ Louise Hay's *You Can Heal Your Life* includes a brilliant reference chart that lists physical ailments and the spiritual root cause.

- ♥ DreamMoods.com or a good-quality dream book can help with interpreting symbols.

- ♥ Working with oracles (see Chapter Eight), which typically come with their own reference book.

Recap

♥ Messages are typically symbolic but may occasionally be literal.

♥ Look for symbolism, hidden or double meanings, colours, plays on words, animals, numbers and personal references.

♥ Additional resources and references, like Google or books, can help with interpreting. Always filter through your own heart.

♥ Create your own reference library of personalised interpretations.

♥ Repeat the Asking, Receiving and Interpreting stages to clarify a message. This may take time.

♥ Review all the messages you've received and recorded in your journal to date, and interpret them.

♥ Your daily ritual can now expand to include:
  – developing an interpretation index
  – layering the practice by posing new supporting questions and repeating the ARIA Method for more insights and clarity.

CHAPTER SIX

ACTING

We now enter the final stage of the ARIA Method: acting. Not just taking any action, but *Inspired Action* as required by Universal Law. As you've seen, some messages are simple to receive, interpret and therefore act on. You feel unwell, you rest. Your friend pops into your mind, you reach out. But not all actions are so clear. Some you may want to avoid. This is particularly true for the seemingly riskier BSQs than, say, the consequences of resting or phoning a friend. The BSQs concerning our life path and its crossroads may require actions of magnitude or significance. Such actions may remain a little hazy (in which case, go inward). The actions required in response to the smaller, supporting questions may be relatively straightforward.

Some actions will point us inward, while other actions need to be taken in the real world. Not everything requires immediate action. Sometimes the timing will be up to us; at other times the Universe forces our hand. In this chapter, I'll walk you through the dos and don'ts of taking aligned and Inspired Action. Focusing on the *inspired* element, we can figure out what steps we need to take, and when, by simply following our heart. The question now is: are you ready to act?

Yes, No, Maybe

I have a confession … your heart and Four Bodies are very capable of giving you a clear 'yes' or 'no' answer. Please don't hate me! You haven't wasted your time, because everything you've learned to date is needed to create context and meaning for those yes/no answers. Sometimes these yes/no answers are best reserved for the supporting questions, building up to a yes/no answer for a BSQ.

To test this, let's determine your yes and no answers. What is something you already logically know is a definite yes? Perhaps it's a decision you've already confidently made, or an issue or person you feel strongly about. Hold its vibration in your heart, then ask yourself a question where you know the answer is yes, and notice how your heart and Four Bodies feel.

Repeat the process, this time for something you logically already know is a definite no. For example, if you have no intention of travelling first class internationally tomorrow you could ask that question and receive a no (although, if you get a yes, be open to a surprise trip!). Perhaps you'll need to think of someone you are not particularly fond of, or an issue you find abhorrent, and temporarily hold that vibration in your heart. Pose a question you know will garner a strong no response and notice how your heart and Four Bodies feel this time. Record how both the yes and no felt.

My heart's yes is usually felt as a Full Body Yes. I feel aligned, happy, open, warm and excited and my whole body responds positively. A Full Body No usually feels like a contraction, shrinking, tension, a deep dread in the pit of my stomach, or escapes as an audible groan.

Beware: you can experience a yes, and also feel fear. You can experience a no and still have the possibility make logical sense. The Law of Polarity supports this. There is also a world of difference between the groan of a no because the action is hard but necessary, for example, versus the groan of a no because your Four Bodies are literally shuddering at the thought. Spot the difference by repeating steps one, two and three of the ARIA Method.

In the absence of a Full Body Yes or a Full Body No, you have a 'maybe', or at least a 'not yet'. Such a response leads us to recycle through the ARIA Method, asking supporting questions or paying closer attention to the feedback loop. In this instance, the action is pointing us inward until our whole body vibrates in response. The action here is to wait.

Internal or External Actions

We know the Law of Correspondence points us inward to address an outer world misalignment. Using the Mirror Technique, or allowing our Four Bodies to show us the behaviours, thoughts, emotions or energy needing attention, we have, by default, been given *internal actions* to take – sometimes called the 'inner work'.

Inner work is just a fancy way of saying the Inspired Action is giving us an opportunity to turn inward and rework our internal state. The Inspired Action may be to revisit our beliefs, or release stored emotions or navigate deep trauma. Sometimes we know exactly where to start and other times these wounds have festered unattended in our bodies for a reason. Support could look like coaches, mentors, therapists or energy healers who are well placed to help with the specific realignment you may need. If you're not sure where to turn, ask for guidance – then watch who or what materialises as help.

Other times, the action is quite plainly something we need to do in the world around us, or 'outer work'. Make a call, take a class, leave a job, start a business, revamp your style. These external actions are Inspired Actions that are more tangible and measurable in the physical world. Again and again, the feedback loop cycles us through the Inspired Actions in our internal world, creating outer world changes, which we then respond to internally, before the change manifests in the outer world. And on and on it goes.

All of this to say: don't overlook the actions that require introspection. We won't get too much further in the process without it because **if nothing (internally) changes, then nothing (externally) changes.** And yes, resisting the inner work is itself a sign.

The Guidance Cycle

Let's revisit the Guidance Cycle from Chapter One. Addressing the inner world will require clearing, healing and/or restoring so we can become a vibrational match for the outer manifestation we desire. We can start with the Four Bodies, addressing what we discovered to free up energy flow again. Reviewing the language used in your journal, for example, may make it obvious what phase you're in, and you may see those words or phrases repeated in the table below. Consider which phase you might be in, based on the guidance you're receiving or by what you intuitively sense when you read the list below.

INNER WORK	*Clear*	• Let go and release people, places, possessions, weight, behaviours etc. • Review, reframe and refine beliefs, perspectives, identities. • Release stored emotions, trauma work, process grief. • Process stagnant energy in your field, chakras or aura.
	Heal	• Repair relationships, physical ailments, possessions. • Work with a therapist, mentor, coach, energy provider (reiki, kinesiology etc.). • Reframe and replace limiting beliefs, old stories and perspectives with new beliefs, identities.
	Restore	• Physical rest and recovery. • Change your diet and exercise. • Bring energy to a state of overflow. • Use mindfulness, meditation. Find stillness, space and silence so the mind can rest. • Focus on nourishing activities, practices, hobbies and creative pursuits.
OUTER WORK	*Manifest*	• Creating and expressing (see Chapter Ten). • Take more time for activities that feel good, and are aligned. • Spend time with people, places, activities that are a vibrational match. • Build. Create. Design. Produce. Achieve. Do.

Three Threads of Guidance

Just as your guidance will lead you through an ongoing process of clearing, healing, restoring and manifesting, you may also begin to observe that the Inspired Action steps tend to fall into one of three categories, or what I call the Three Threads of Guidance:

- ♥ **Daily intuitive instructions** = small, low-risk instructions and external actions. For example, rest, go to yoga, call that friend. Practical, clear, intuited Inspired Actions most often linked to the supporting questions.

- ♥ **Overarching direction** = big picture and somewhat elusive impressions, often painting a final destination, not the journey. Rarely require immediate action, but lead to additional (mostly internal) actions to reach the big vision or dream. For example, 'I want to help women' or 'I want to support children somehow' may be heart desires, but remain vague in terms of actions. Often linked to the heart's desires.

- ♥ **Healing journey** = a mix of internal and external actions to bring us back into vibrational alignment by actively doing the inner work of the Guidance Cycle. Typically linked to the BSQs.

Time to review your journal notes thus far. Can you identify which threads of guidance you've received? If you're stuck ruminating about an overarching direction, allow it to be there, and come back to the smaller, seemingly unrelated intuitive instructions and inner work. Everything is connected and will eventually shift and change in a time and rhythm all of its own.

Change Your Diet, Buy a House

A few years back, my husband and I wanted to buy a house for our growing family (our heart's core desire was to put down roots). Taking all the real-world external actions, we saved a deposit, trawled real estate websites, visited open homes, made offers. The more we got knocked back, the more supporting questions I asked. The answer surprised me: 'Change your diet, buy a house.'

At first glance that seemed preposterous. Then it clicked. For some time, I received (and, I'll admit, ignored) intuitive instructions to change my diet. Frustrated, my head couldn't immediately see the link of my diet to the practicalities of buying a house. My heart, though, recognised that without acting on the other threads, I'd never reach my destination. Changing my diet would help me align my Four Bodies, thus changing my vibration and, in turn, realigning my energy with my intention to buy a house. We still live in the house we bought a few weeks later.

What appears to be completely unrelated is, indeed, related. The Three Threads of Guidance interweave. **Although you may ask for guidance in one area, you may receive instructions to take Inspired Action elsewhere. We can't pick and choose which guidance we act on.** Everything is connected.

Timing

Many times, I've had a Universal green light, but got stalled, or was delayed, and no amount of external action would translate to change. The frustration of life not running to our mind's plans and timeframes is all too real. Clock-based timing is not the same as time beyond the physical. There is an element of divine timing and, according to the Law of Rhythm, everything has its own natural timing that won't be dictated by our man-made clocks. Stretching this concept a little further, what if you could actually align your frequency to be a match for divine timing? By 'becoming one with time', you can flow with the slipstream rather than fighting the current.

To help me explain, think of a time when you were running late to an event or meeting. Your mind was probably acutely aware of your tardiness, a physical panic may have set in which subsequently would have set a new dominant frequency. Did it feel like everything else slowed down around you? Traffic piled up. Lights stayed red. You got stuck behind a Sunday driver (or a truck with oversized tyres). With all your awareness, energy and attention on the vibration of there 'not being enough time', or repeating that you 'would never get there in time', that's what you created. The Universe matched your vibration.

But the opposite can also be true. What about when you lose track of time? Maybe there's been a time where you were in the flow with a creative project, or whiling away an afternoon with a loved one. This is an example of when we are aligned with time, things flow and our thinking is not interfering with the natural rhythm of things. *This* is the state of alignment we will want to achieve in order to act on our intuition, without forcing or pushing it before the time is right. To do this, we must act without attachment to it falling into place in a linear, chronological way according to the logic of time.

Perceived Urgency and 'Bigness'

Many people report their Full Body Yes also feels like a rush of urgency, that action must be taken *now*. What we perceive as urgent may be more an indication of importance, rather than a need for speed. I often say spirit doesn't have a clock and soul doesn't have a calendar – the Universe flows according to its own rhythm. **Just because it feels urgent doesn't mean you have to take immediate action.** Tune in a little deeper and ask about the timing and perceived urgency with your supporting questions. The exercise at the end of this chapter may also help.

An overwhelming sense of 'bigness' is often associated with the answers to our BSQ, especially when it comes to a life-altering decision or career change. It can feel B-I-G. Stiflingly so. Having a sense of 'bigness' to the answer or action is also a good sign, not one to be deterred by. Like urgency, 'bigness' may highlight the incredible importance or alignment with your life's purpose. Break it down with supporting questions for more manageable, bite-sized Inspired Actions.

No Bargains or Guarantees

And now for the small print: just because your heart says yes doesn't mean it will be smooth sailing or happy ever after. Our intuition is designed to help us navigate our life path, which means we will move into new situations that help us grow, often through challenge or grittiness. I explain this in more detail in *You Already Know*, but suffice to say here, there is always a reason you're led somewhere, if only to bring you back into vibrational alignment. The Law of Divine Oneness says everything and everyone is connected; the Law of Perpetual Transmutation of Energy ensures you are (and your energy is) constantly evolving; and the Law of Rhythm says it will happen with a timing all of its own. We can't outsmart it. We can't negotiate a better deal, or promise actions when, and only when, the Universe delivers something first. The Law of Compensation says if you go all in with Inspired Action (even if you're making the 'wrong' step), you will be rewarded. Life will come rushing in to support you in a way your mind cannot control, fathom or outsmart – so you at least need to crack a window, or fling open the door to let it in. Let the Universe surprise you (and see what happens when you set that as your vibrational base level).

Avoidance, Fear and Resistance

Even when there is a clear course of intuitive Inspired Action, the head may still fight against it. We may fear the repercussions of that action. Our fear may stem from an outdated belief, a lack of self-esteem or a perceived risk of abandonment (or any other type of fear, for that matter). These internal clues can then trigger a new line of questioning with the ARIA Method, this time with supporting questions around the fear, its source and how to grow through it. While doing the inner work, we hold the heart's core desire and continue to expand it. Both can be present – it's the Law of Polarity.

In this way, we begin to relate to our fears, avoidance and resistance as tools of deeper self-awareness and discovery. **The ARIA Method is not just about getting what you want – it's also about the *how*.** The ARIA Method is not just a navigational tool for external action (autocorrect tried to make that 'eternal' action), but also as a tool for self-awareness, inner growth and transformation.

The Next Right Step

Whether you're trying to make sense of the instructions you already have, or just want to try this as part of your daily practice, a great line of questioning for action is this:

What is the next immediate step I need to take?

Bonus points if you include inner and outer immediate steps.

Following the same ARIA process, pose this question in your heart and put yourself into a position of receiving. Notice anything your body fires back at you, or any other impressions that arise. Interpret them. Then, with nothing else left to do, *take that step.*

Recap

- ♥ Inspired Actions are the intuitive actions we must take to align with our hearts and the Universe.

- ♥ Become familiar your heart's 'yes', 'no' and 'maybe' and how they're different from your head's 'yes', 'no' and 'maybe'.

- ♥ A sense of urgency and 'bigness' may be more about importance than rapid action.

- ♥ Some Inspired Actions require outward actions – make a call, visit a place, make this change – while some require internal actions – reframe your beliefs, clean up your diet, align your energy. Both are important.

- ♥ Guidance may fall into one of three categories: daily intuitive instructions, overarching direction, and healing journey. They are connected, and the smaller daily steps unravel the bigger picture.

♥ If you're struggling to act on your intuition, this can alert you to areas to explore via the **ARIA** Method, to understand the resistance or avoidance and how to overcome it.

♥ Your daily practice can now expand to include:
- reflecting on the actions to determine what steps are needed
- doing the inner work, as required
- making the outer world changes, as required.

PART ONE RECAP

- ♥ Universal Laws govern how we interact with the Universe.

- ♥ Your head and heart have competing agendas, but they need to work together.

- ♥ Your heart is an antenna receiving guidance and transmitting desires, via their vibrations.

- ♥ As we exchange vibrations with the Universe, and vice versa, we are part of a feedback loop that shows us if we are aligned with our heart's desires, or if internal realignment is required.

- ♥ To understand the feedback loop, we use the ARIA Method:
  - Asking for what we want (through energy, intention, vibration and focused awareness)
  - Receiving (in response to our thoughts, energy, intention and vibration)
  - Interpreting the signs, symbols and symptoms we receive
  - Acting on that data, to realign or manifest more.

- ♥ We have a combiner that merges the heart's signals with our Four Bodies' signals.

- ♥ The Universe also delivers external signs and messengers.

- ♥ Our intuition translates the signs and combined antenna signals into a language the head can understand.

- ♥ The ARIA Method can be applied in one sitting, or over many days, weeks or months. That's why we need an ongoing process, not just a fleeting Q&A.

- ♥ The Guidance Cycle will continue to guide us inward to realign by clearing, healing or restoring, in order to manifest our heart's desire.

PART TWO

THE TOOLKIT

CHAPTER SEVEN

JOURNALING

Journaling was single-handedly the best thing I did when I began working with my intuition and consciously creating my dream life. Hopefully you've seen the benefit so far in recording your progress and intuitive impressions. While that will remain the cornerstone of this work, we now introduce an array of journaling techniques to strengthen your intuition and deepen your self-awareness. Having all your notes, questions, impressions and interpretations in one place will make reviewing your intuitive hunches easier. Through this process, you will develop 'proof', putting the naysaying mind back in its rightful place. Journaling reveals patterns over time, deepening your self-awareness and inner work, clearly revealing where the feedback loop is steering you.

Experimenting with the tools and techniques in this chapter, your heart will decide what it needs to work with at any given time, or which tool might be better for a particular goal. After fifteen years of dedicated journaling using the techniques in this book, I have some tips and tricks to help you streamline the process, including what to do if you aren't so keen on writing. Over that time, one of the biggest surprises to me is where I've landed on the paper versus digital debate.

Paper or Digital

Since the time I learned to write, I've kept a journal. More specifically, the following techniques have filled the pages of more than 250 journals. Nothing beats the drawl of my favourite pen's ink across a fresh sheet of paper – and yet, this writer has found herself ensconced in the digital camp. Of late, I have found more pros in the digital column. Yes, I created a pro and con list, which I share below. Feel free to add your own thoughts – your heart might land somewhere else.

	Pro	Con
PAPER	Pro • Luxurious (especially for a writer) • Papyrophilia is real • Lower starting cost	Con • You can't hyperlink • Difficult to locate specifics across multiple journals • Storage is an issue • May require cross-referencing or filing system • Can be bulky to carry with you
DIGITAL	Pro • Easy to carry with you • Transfers across devices • Environmentally friendly • You can hyperlink, copy and paste, insert images • Easy digital storage	Con • It's not paper! • More expensive up-front costs, if you don't already have a tablet and apps

Smart device apps like GoodNotes allow you to have a digital journal on your tablet, then write directly onto it, annotating the pages, highlighting, hyperlinking, sketching, right there on the page – then save it on the cloud. With hundreds of journals stored in my office, this was a massive win. Digital also allows you to save your files with keywords, tag content, and the like, making it easier to go back and find something specific you wrote. And, because of the cloud, it can be accessed across your devices, meaning you can take it with you everywhere – handy for when you notice signs in your day-to-day life.

Sticking with paper is absolutely fine too. Neither is right or wrong. You can change your mind later or even develop a hybrid system all of your own. Let your heart decide.

What to Include in Your Journal

An example journal page is included at the end of this chapter (similar downloads are available at my website helenjacobs.co). Looking at the sample, you'll notice there are a few key things to record in each entry:

- ♥ the date (and sometimes the time)
- ♥ an overview of what's happening in your life (dot points are ok)
- ♥ the current BSQ
- ♥ any observations, impressions and notes from your practice.

Sometimes this high-level entry will suffice. Other times, you'll want blank pages for the deeper, more explorative journaling practices I share in this chapter. (By the way, this can be another advantage of the digital system as you can insert and replicate blank pages, lined pages, grid pages and more straight into the journal, as and where you need them, so the journal is always designed exactly as you need it.) Let's now maximise your journaling practice to develop your intuition and clarify your heart's desires.

Journaling Practices

On the following pages I'll share my favourite journaling techniques to support your intuitive adventure. Depending on what you're exploring through your morning ritual, you might work with one technique for a while, then intuitively change it up. Time may be a factor, influencing which technique you use when. At a minimum, please ensure you still capture your observations and impressions each day, and include longer-form journaling when time permits. In Chapter Eleven you'll develop a plan for this too.

Stream of Consciousness

This journaling technique essentially invites you to write every thought as it passes through your mind, without censoring. Perfect before meditation, this technique clears the mind chatter ahead of your practice. Stream of consciousness writing may result in you capturing your grocery or to do list; it's not about perfecting the world's greatest prose. Don't contemplate what you're writing, just get anything and everything down on the page, without pausing. Eventually, this technique will reveal the thoughts repetitively running through your mind. Such free-form journaling is great for the clearing phase of the Guidance Cycle, and can help clarify your BSQ.

Julia Cameron, author of *The Artist's Way*, recommends what she calls morning pages, whereby you commit to three pages of stream of consciousness writing every morning upon waking. At times, I've included this in my own daily practice, especially when I'm unearthing or exploring something in the clearing or healing phases. Over time and with review, recurring themes and patterns emerge, as well as your daily intuitive instructions, right there on the page. It's a great tool for eliciting actions – just make sure your heart agrees with.

Automatic Writing

Not to be confused with stream of consciousness writing, automatic writing allows a higher consciousness than your own to write. While stream of consciousness writing allows your *thoughts* to roam free, automatic writing allows the *heart* to reign. Although this technique can take some practice, it can elicit some powerful results.

Here, the heart must take the lead. It's best done following meditation (explored more in Chapter Nine), so you've reached a very centred state. Then pose a question (whether the BSQ or a supporting question) and allow your heart to answer, not your mind. Because you've just meditated, I'd recommend taking pen to paper – possibly even with eyes still closed! – and just allowing the words to come, to be felt, without thought. When I first began this practice, only one or two words would arrive and often scribbles filled the page, rather than anything useful. With committed practice, this technique now fills the majority of my journal pages with key intuitive information my head wasn't able to access on its own.

A clever trick to bypass the mind: write your question with your usual writing hand (dominant hand) and then answer using your non-dominant hand. Yes, it will be messy, but what you can decipher may just surprise you!

Future Scripting

This is one of my favourite journaling techniques for both manifesting and aligning my intention, energy and thoughts with my heart's core desire. This exercise is best done after connecting with your heart space and tuning into what is there or working with the Expanding the Vibration of Your Heart's Desire exercise from Chapter Three.

Dream of a future point, where a future version of you is experiencing everything your heart desires. Then write from that point of view. Ask your future self to write, describing what it's like there, especially how it *feels*. As your future self writes, they describe the scenery, how they feel, who they're with, what they're doing, what they're grateful for, possibly even the Inspired Actions that helped them get there. As much detail and *feeling* as possible goes onto the page. Yes, this feels like daydreaming and imaginary play, but the Universe doesn't know the difference; it just responds to the dominant vibration.

Future scripting won't work as a one-hit wonder. Frequent connection with this vibration will enhance your ability to attract it. If time permits, rewrite the script daily, or at least read it once a day. Alternatively, record yourself reading it aloud then listen to it as often as possible (and this has an added bonus that will make more sense after exploring the healing vibrations in your own voice in Chapter Ten).

Point of View Writing

Like future scripting, this technique doesn't require frequently connecting with the vibration of your vision (although that would improve your success with manifesting). Instead, this technique helps provide intuitive 'proof'. Like future scripting, it requires you write to yourself from a different perspective, but not just a future version – it could be a past version, or some other point of view. Here are some ideas:

- ❤ Connect with yourself nearing the end of your life and write yourself a letter from that perspective. What are you proud of? Grateful for? Who were the key people in your life? What do you regret not having done? What were your biggest accomplishments? What should you not have wasted time worrying about?

- ❤ Connect with your younger self, exploring how they felt and dealt with certain moments in their life. What does this version of you need for healing?

- ❤ Write to yourself from the perspective of your BSQ.

- ❤ Write to yourself from the perspective of a particularly strong emotion or memory.

- ❤ Write to yourself from the perspective of one (or all) of your Four Bodies.

My husband and I use a version of this practice annually, on our anniversary. We each write ourselves a letter from our future self, who details everything that transpires in the year ahead. Once finished, without reading or sharing, we place the letters straight into envelopes, seal them, and put them aside until next year's anniversary. Then we share and read them. It's uncanny how much will have come to fruition – and how we had tapped into each other's future too.

Journal Prompts

For those who aren't naturally expressive via writing, journaling prompts are a great kickstart to your inner exploration. And if you're not naturally inclined to write, many of these can be explored through more creative means (more on that in Chapter Ten). Several journal prompts have been scattered throughout the book, including the sample supporting questions on page 41. The tables and exercises throughout the book are also great prompts. Other ways to kickstart your journaling include:

- ♥ Take an oracle card (see Chapter Eight) and journal about what it represents for you.

- ♥ Open a personal development book (or just this one!) at a random page, then journal about the topic there.

- ♥ Choose an affirmation and explore your experience with it.

- ♥ Use today's date and reflect on this time last year (or future script to this time next year).

♥ Use your heart's desire as a jumping-off point.

Other Types of Journaling

Specific tools are useful at certain times, perhaps during a particular phase of the Guidance Cycle, or when you're working on manifesting something and need to clear the way to receive it. Consider the examples below and draw on them when you feel intuitively guided to:

♥ **Dream journaling** – recording and interpreting your dreams, where so much symbolism and subconscious and intuitive data resides. I share an exercise in Chapter Eight.

♥ **Inner child journaling** – as mentioned earlier, connecting with your younger self and exploring their needs, perhaps writing from their perspective regarding a significant moment in time, or more generally.

♥ **Gratitude journaling** – recording a list every day of (new) people and things you're grateful for, as you started doing in Chapter Four. Bonus points for journaling about *why* you're grateful.

♥ **Visual or creative journaling** – akin to scrapbooking, this visual process uses images, collages, paints, pens etc. to pour your heart onto the page. This can be done on paper, or digitally, as a form of creative self-expression (which we explore more deeply in Chapter Ten). This is also a great tool for vision boarding, helping you visually connect with your heart's desire and intentions.

More Tips, Tricks and Tools

After utilising these techniques daily for at least fifteen years, I have a few tips and tricks to share that may help streamline your own systems. Your own heart, of course, will build its own preferences over time too.

Colour Codes

Regardless of whether you're using paper or digital, it's useful to develop a system to capture repeating patterns and themes. On paper, this may look like a personalised shorthand in the margins, annotating where there are questions, answers, card readings and the like. Consider what this might look like across multiple physical journals. For me, a multitude of coloured post-its adorned the pages, with shorthand code for different topics in each journal. Highlighters or coloured pens are perfect for marking up your impressions and findings. In a digital journal, this process becomes a lot easier and doesn't require multiple tools – just a filing system that works for you.

Cataloguing System

Again, this is also easier in a digital system, but as your journal collection grows, you'll want a way to catalogue the magic you have in those pages. They will be rich with intuitive data, self-awareness patterns, signs and symbols.

To Keep, or Not to Keep

Of course, there's no need to keep everything and there can be therapeutic (and energetic) benefits in letting the vibration of all of this go (and yes, this all has its own frequency, too, which you may not want to keep forever). It's not unusual to want to dispose of old journals during the clearing or healing phase of the Guidance Cycle. Most of my free-form journaling ends up in the annual fire, very symbolically burning through the old. But in terms of guidance – that stuff is pure gold and I won't destroy mine anytime soon. Let your heart guide you.

Tools

For paper journals, lined are my favourite, but there are many options available. A5 seems to be just the right size to pop in your handbag and lightweight enough for this too. For digital, I work on my iPad and use both the GoodNotes and Nebo apps. I have an Apple pencil which is the only other tool I need. I won't always carry my iPad with me, but both apps are synced to my phone, which is never too far from me.

Journal Your Journey

Regardless of the techniques and tools you experiment with, the following below will guide you on how to weave journaling into your daily ritual. By the end of the book, you'll be able to apply longer journaling practices over months and years too. Also included is the example journal page I mentioned earlier.

A SIMPLE STEP-BY-STEP GUIDE TO DAILY JOURNALING TO ACCESS YOUR INTUITION

1. Sit quietly and tune into your heart space, taking a few deep breaths into that space.

2. With journal and pen handy (the example journal page opposite will be useful, or just annotate your page yourself):

   – Record the date.

   – Write what's in your heart today.

   – Write what's on your mind today.

   – Record any impressions and insights you've received in the past 24 hours, and how you interpret them. (You might like to add your interpretations to your reference index.)

   – Choose a journal prompt (from this chapter, or from the sample supporting questions on page 41).

   – Explore this prompt in your journal using one of the techniques in this chapter.

   – If you feel called to, and have time, you may like to use other journaling techniques here to explore personal topics.

3. If you have time, you may want to reflect on your journal entry, annotating any key phrases, messages and insights.

EXAMPLE JOURNAL PAGE

Date:

Overview/what's happening in my life right now:

→ on my mind   → in my heart

BSQs	Supporting questions

Observations, impressions, signs (Four Bodies):

Recap

- ♥ Include journaling in your morning ritual, at a bare minimum to record impressions and manifestations. As needed, expand using the techniques in this chapter, choosing the ones appropriate to the focus of your inner work.

- ♥ Experiment with paper and digital journals. Whichever you choose, develop a personal system for reviewing and storing your notes.

- ♥ Date and keep everything – it's all proof to appease your mind.

- ♥ If you're not so much a writer, at least write dot points for this process, and instead focus on creative expression through other means (as we'll explore in Chapter Ten).

CHAPTER EIGHT

ORACLES

Throughout history and across cultures and religions, people have worked with divination tools to connect with something beyond themselves, seeking guidance and insight. That same element of history and culture may influence which tools are easily accepted, and which are not. Depending on your own beliefs and comfort levels, such tools can provide additional layers and context to the messages and manifestations received.

By definition, an oracle is someone or something through which guidance is delivered. In this chapter, I introduce tools like oracle and tarot cards, bibliomancy, pendulums, muscle testing, dream interpretation and more, although we've already seen how to get answers through signs, symbols and messengers. There's no need to venture into anything you're uncomfortable with. Just check in with your own heart to feel what you're drawn to working with. Experiment with the suggestions, or perhaps others from your own culture, religion and background. Find what works for you. The point here is to be able to add additional insight and information to your daily ritual in a way that adds proof beyond your own logic.

Usually at this point, questions are raised about whether these sorts of tools are truly oracles, or really just a manifestation of the answers sought. My answer is: a little of both. Your dominant vibration will be reflected in the card or message received, but we counter this by being very clear about what (and how) we ask. Working with open, supporting questions geared towards clarity and context attracts similar answers. The nature of your question or BSQ may influence the card you turn (or more precisely, perhaps, how you interpret it) but your *dominant* frequency will prevail. If your dominant vibration is a willingness to learn, grow and gain new perspectives, then your oracle's answer will be in that vein. However, if you simply want them to support a predetermined point of view, oracles may not be for you. Setting an intention (and dominant vibration) for higher guidance when working with these divination tools will guide what you attract.

Regardless of the tool, the goal remains the same: set your intention, ask your question, receive and interpret the messages, then act. Combined with what you learn through your journaling and observing your Four Bodies, as well as any signs and external messages, you can layer meanings and messages, manifesting what you couldn't have orchestrated yourself.

Let's now explore the ways you can use such tools to intuit and manifest what's in your heart.

Set Your Intention

Setting an intention for working with and receiving guidance from oracles requires a focusing of energy, so your thoughts, beliefs, emotions, feelings and actions are all aligned. Over time, working with the ARIA Method and its feedback loop, this alignment of mind–body–spirit will manifest and become your dominant state. Until then, it's important to set an intention each and every time you work with your preferred oracle tool.

Often, intention-setting is confused with an end goal or a *mental* act of determining some result or action. However, because we know there are Four Bodies, not just one, our intention-setting is going to focus on the physical, mental, emotional and energetic layers. **Intention-setting is less about the goal or outcome, and more about the vibration *behind* it. Successful intention-setting aligns the vibration with which you *begin* your journey with that you desire at the *end*.** To manifest and attract the end state, we need to set that as the intention to begin with. Then we ask all Four Bodies to align with that same frequency. In fact, you've already been aligning with your heart's core desire, your intention, since the Expanding the Vibration of Your Heart's Desire exercise in Chapter Three.

Just as you set your heart's desire, you can now set a smaller or supporting intention while working with your chosen oracle. This requires a move beyond *willingness* into a deep belief, inner knowing and trust that your answers will come. Hopefully your progress to date has supported this. Revisit the Asking for Your Heart's Desires exercise in Chapter Three, this time setting your intention to work with oracles. Then refer to the box following to ensure all Four Bodies are aligned with that intention.

ALIGNING YOUR FOUR BODIES
WITH YOUR INTENTION

Physical intention: Do your actions support this intention? Are you working with the Universe, listening to your heart and maintaining a daily ritual?

Mental intention: Your thoughts and beliefs about this intention will show you if you are open to it manifesting or not. Have you moved beyond willingness? Have you worked through any fear or old beliefs?

Emotional intention: Old, stored emotions may block the flow of your receiving, like boulders in a river. Are past hurts keeping you closed? Are you guarding your heart? Blocking in one area of your life can affect other areas.

Spiritual intention: Does your internal state resonate with your intention? Are you prepared to reach this vibration and expand it in your being, aligning yourself to the possibilities before you?

Come to your daily ritual with an intention for the practice, and run that through your Four Bodies too. When you next sit for your daily practice, come back to your intention for the sitting, then add a form of oracle into your practice.

Let's look at the tools you might like to explore and add into your practice.

Oracle Cards

An oracle card is usually part of a deck of cards designed to deliver guidance and messages. These are different from tarot cards, which I'll explain below. Working with oracle cards was a game changer for me, because they delivered additional messages that added context to my intuition and also additional inner work to help my manifestations. They were a great tool for my supporting questions and helped me understand myself.

Although I worked with various decks, I never found one I truly resonated with until I created my own deck, The Little Sage Oracle Cards. That said, I still have many other decks in my personal collection which I'll work with if I feel drawn to them. Some decks focus on certain topics or themes, so you might gravitate towards different decks during different phases in your life (or when dealing with different BSQs). You can also have a lot of fun working across multiple decks from different creators – and when the same message is revealed across those decks, you know you've got your answer!

Like everything else under the Law of Vibration, oracle card decks vibrate at their own frequency (as all divination tools do). This can be influenced by the creator, their intention when creating the decks, or just the messages and themes of the decks themselves. When selecting which cards to work with (or not), consider the deck's vibration and if it's a vibrational match for you and your intention. Pay attention to any discomfort with certain decks – or all decks, for that matter. Consider whether the discomfort stems from the vibration of the particular cards in question, or whether it's the entire genre (that is, all oracle cards). When shopping for (or even borrowing) a deck, notice how your combined antennas (the heart and Four Bodies) respond. Does the energy feel open, loving, inviting, or does it feel like a heavier or darker energy? Interpret that message and then act accordingly.

Oracle Cards versus Tarot Cards

Tarot cards are quite different in energy and function to oracle cards, having first originated in the 1400s alongside other divination practices of that time. It's an energy I don't personally vibe with – but you might! Like playing cards, tarot has four suits of cards, each featuring a particular theme. The cards are divided into what is called the minor arcana (themes that are specific to the individual) and the major arcana (themes of a collective or shared nature). All cards are numbered, providing a system to outline stages of a pathway or journey that the user may be on. Each card includes detailed images, rich with symbolism, especially the more traditional decks.

Because of the history of the cards, there's a lot of talk about death (hopefully more symbolic than literal!) and some of the symbolism can be a little 'heavier' in energy, although many more modern decks seem to counteract that. Incredibly popular, tarot is loved by many and you may be one of them.

Experiment and see what you're drawn to. By the way, you can use an ordinary deck of playing cards in a similar way.

Affirmation Cards

Affirmation cards serve up a completely different energy to both tarot and oracle cards. These cards offer positively framed statements that, when recited, can elicit a particular vibration and intention for the user. Affirmations can help reframe thinking and beliefs, and can set an intention (and vibration) to improve one's outlook. Many decks will also include imagery, but don't typically come with reference books to help interpret it.

Like oracle and tarot cards, there are many affirmation decks on the market, each with its own frequency. If oracle or tarot cards don't resonate for you, affirmation cards may be a perfect starting point. These can be used as the creator intended, or as a journaling prompt each day, or as an answer to any question you may be asking.

Other Divination Tools

Beyond the use of cards, a whole host of oracle options are available. A brief smattering of examples follow. Don't forget, if you'd like to find your own, work with the ARIA Method to ask for the perfect solution, then receive the answer that comes.

Bibliomancy

This is a fancy term for what is essentially flipping to a random line on a random page in a random book and allowing what you read there to provide guidance. When I first started exploring my psychic and intuitive abilities, bibliomancy was introduced during a workshop I attended. I didn't attach much weight to it, but participated with an open heart and mind anyway. At the time, my BSQ was about leaving my PR role, and what job I should explore next. Flipping to the page at random, I landed on a passage about trading in a corporate power suit. Of course, I didn't literally wear such outfits, but the symbolism was clear nevertheless. By the end of that workshop, I did receive the answers I needed – the psychic leading the workshop saw my natural ability and suggested I just start giving readings. You now know how that turned out!

Since you're reading this book, I'll hazard a guess that you have amassed a collection of self-help and personal development books. Let's just say I had a hunch! Your collection is about to be put to a whole new use in the exercise below.

USING YOUR BOOKS AS AN ORACLE – BIBLIOMANCY

1. Take a deep breath, tune into your heart space and allow a heart-led question to arise.

2. Hold the energy or vibration of that question in your heart space. You may even like to say it aloud.

3. You may now like to intuitively select a book to work with, if you haven't already.

4. Take the book off the shelf, close your eyes and fan through the pages of your chosen book and stop when it feels right in your heart.

5. Allow your fingers (not your eyes) to move over the page and stop where they feel it's right to.

6. Then open your eyes and read the sentence, phrase or paragraph where your finger landed.

7. Record both the question and the message in your journal.

8. You can interpret it here, if it makes sense, or perhaps use other tools now to add to your meaning.

Pendulums

Years ago, while I was lying on the couch heavily pregnant, my mum took my engagement ring, placed it on a necklace and swung it over my swollen belly to determine the gender of my unborn child. Perhaps you've played a similar baby shower game? If yes, then you've worked with pendulums before.

A pendulum has a weighted point on an arm (or string) that allows for movement at the weighted point when held still at the top of the string. Used as a divination tool, the way the pendulum moves in response to questions posed can provide answers – handy when asking questions about what actions to take and when, as explored in Chapter Six.

You can purchase beautiful crystal pendulums or simply make your own by threading a ring with an evenly weighted point (like a stone or gem) onto a piece of string or necklace à la my mum. Hold your pendulum at the top of the string, ensuring your elbow is resting on a flat surface (like a sturdy table) and that you're lightly gripping the top of your string. You're now ready to ask your pendulum for answers – but first, program your pendulum with practice questions. Do this by asking questions you logically already know the answer to; for example:

- ♥ 'Is my name (insert your name)?' (or try with a name that isn't yours!)

- ♥ 'Do I have blue hair?'

- ♥ 'Am I currently at (insert location or address)?'

Allow the pendulum to begin swinging of its own volition – *do not force it!* The pendulum will begin moving in distinct ways, with different movements representing 'yes' or 'no' answers (you might also get a 'maybe'). You can also ask the pendulum 'Show me yes' then 'Show me no.' Typically, the pendulum will swing back and forth, left to right, or even in a circle. Your 'yes' and 'no' may change from sitting to sitting, so it's a good idea to check each time you wish to use it. Once you have differentiated what is 'yes' or 'no' (and even a 'maybe'), you can ask your heart-led questions.

A word of caution: clearly set your intention before this activity, intending to only work with positive energy. This is one activity that has got a bad rap over the years and it can take on murky energy if you haven't carefully set your intention for the vibration you want to work with.

Muscle Testing

If pendulums push your comfort zone, perhaps muscle testing is a better fit. Used in kinesiology, muscle testing allows the physical body to respond to questions (like a human pendulum), by harnessing the energy stored within it. A trained kinesiologist is your best port of call, but I've included a version below that a kinesiologist friend shared with me that's a great self-testing tool.

MUSCLE TESTING FOR YES/NO QUESTIONS

1. Take both hands and bring the thumbs and index fingers of each hand together.

2. Now, interlock them, so each set of finger and thumb makes a circle and the two circles interlock like links on a chain.

3. Test what yes and no are for you by asking questions you know the answer to and then trying to pull the finger-thumb circle apart. For example, a 'yes' may keep the fingers locked, but a 'no' may spring one of the locks open, releasing the fingers.

4. Without forcing this, ask your questions to reveal the yes or no answer.

Dream Interpretation

While not strictly a divination tool, our nightly escapades hold a world of guidance. Following the ARIA Method, we can ask for guidance before we fall asleep, receive it in our dreams, then interpret and act on the messages when we wake.

The types of dreams I'm particularly interested in fall into a few categories:

- ♥ Typical nightly dreams, of which you have up to five, subconsciously processing the events of the past 24–72 hours.

- ♥ A spirit visitation, where a deceased loved one or guiding being may bring a message.

- ♥ A soul encounter, where your soul meets with another soul on the astral plane. These are quite rare, and not to be confused with a typical nightly dream where someone features.

You will know the difference between the first and last two types of dreams by the way they *feel*. Spirit visitations in a dream will likely never be forgotten – and I should know, as it is one such dream after my aunt passed away that completely altered my life's trajectory (I talk more about this in *You*

Already Know, if it piques your interest). You don't need to have this kind of experience, though. Your regular nightly dreams hold a great deal of information about your current situation, guiding you to heal, release, forgive and more. Here's one process for interpreting a typical nightly dream, with a simple example.

THE ARIA METHOD FOR DREAMS

1. Before bed, place your daily ritual tools on your bedside table, so they're on hand in the morning, or move them to your sacred space immediately upon waking.

2. Before sleep, formulate your question. Bring the energy of that question into your heart space and hold a gentle awareness of that frequency as you drift off to sleep (you won't want to be distracted before bed, and the use of meditation music or gentle sleep aids like essential oils or massage may help).

3. Hold the intention that you will remember your dream upon waking.

4. Go to sleep. Enjoy your dreams. Receive.

5. Immediately upon waking, grab your journal and record anything you remember from the dream, even if it's just the emotion you wake with. The simple act of recalling your dream can encourage more to be remembered. Record everything.

6. Review what you've written, and make a dot point list of all the symbols in the dream – the people, places, objects, colours, emotions, *everything*.

7. Applying your interpretation skills from Chapter Five, assign a meaning beside each symbol (add these to your personal reference index, too). DreamMoods.com, a dream book or even Google will be particularly useful here. For people, list three describing words for them (don't overthink it), then consider what it says about *you*.

8. Now rewrite the dream sequence, this time inserting each symbol's meanings rather than the symbol itself – see the example below.

9. Re-read what you've written and see what message your dream holds for you.

EXAMPLE DREAM INTERPRETATION

What I remember of my dream sequence:
I dreamt my husband and I were at a party for my birthday. We wanted to leave but couldn't find our car. Then we were driving home, but my husband drove and I was in the back seat.

Symbols and meanings:
Husband: loving, caring, loyal
Party: enjoy yourself, socialise (but it's mine, so appreciation for me – but I want to leave, so perhaps avoiding appreciating and celebrating myself)

Car: how I'm navigating life (couldn't find it to begin with), drive, ambition
Driving: someone else in control of the driving
Back seat: couldn't control the driving

Example dream rewrite and interpretation:
My (loving, caring, loyal part of myself) and I (needed to socialise and enjoy and appreciate myself) but we (avoided celebrating me), and couldn't find (my drive and ambition). Then, we were (navigating my life), but my (loving, caring, loyal part of myself) was in control and I was (no longer in control) of my own life path.

A note for the parents among us often woken by children at inopportune times: if you can't spend time writing all this out, try recording what you remember as a voice note on your phone, or, better yet, use a voice to text option. That way you won't forget the details of the dream, and you can interpret it with gusto when time (and children) permit. The weekly practice you'll establish in Chapter Eleven would be a perfect time to catch up.

Other Tools

Astrology, numerology, runes, lunar cycles, your menstrual cycle, even regular playing cards, can all provide ways of accessing additional guidance. Try setting an intention to manifest the perfect oracle, then notice who or what shows up. You may feel drawn to different support tools at different times (which is also worth observing and noting). Don't forget, life's messengers will also turn up as an external source of guidance.

Working with Oracles

Try the exercise below, then add it into your toolkit. For this exercise you'll need some sort of oracle cards, or bibliomancy could also work here.

WORKING WITH ORACLES

1. Centre yourself in your heart space and set your intention for this exercise in working with your chosen oracle.

2. Sit in stillness and silence, tune into your body and notice what is present. If time permits, include a meditation here.

3. Pose the question to the oracle (including both the specific question and the *feeling* of that question) – then flip to a page, turn a card or two (or whichever tool you're using).

4. What's the first thing you notice about this message? What does it tell you?

5. Interpret the message. Is it literal or symbolic? Interpret the symbolic meaning yourself before consulting any reference book included with your support tool (if there is one).

6. Look at any images, phrases – does something here catch your eye? Work with the interpretation tools in Chapter Five.

7. Perhaps the message doesn't make sense yet. You can repeat this process by asking for more clarification, or allow the question to remain open during the day and observe what other messages, signs etc. turn up.

8. Be sure to record your question and findings in your journal, adding to your interpretation index.

Recap

♥ Your personal vibration influences the flow of answers and opportunities to you. Set your intention (and vibration) for what you attract to be geared towards self-awareness and personal growth, as well as manifesting your heart's desires.

♥ When setting your intention, be clear about the type of energy you are inviting in.

♥ Stay open and curious, noticing the array of answers and solutions that come to you through your oracles and life's messengers. Observe with non-attachment and non-judgement (meditation helps – see the next chapter).

♥ Experiment with different oracles and divination tools.

♥ Include some form of oracle guidance in your daily ritual, allowing for it to change over time, as and if needed.

CHAPTER NINE

MEDITATION

Discussing meditation can make people squirm. Are you squirming? Perhaps it's the frequency that arises because we know we're *meant* to meditate but don't really want to, or don't have enough time, or can't sit still, or the mind just won't quit. These reasons are precisely why you *need* meditation! Such objections are the mind's attempt to control the situation and it won't go down without a fight. Try treating these objections with curiosity, taking them through the ARIA Method to identify how to reframe your beliefs and habits instead.

For the modern woman, the mere suggestion of meditating can feel like yet another thing to add to our already overfull plates. This isn't about finding *more* time in an already full life, but rather reframing existing moments of your day as an opportunity for mindfulness and quiet reflection. If time permits for longer meditative practice, wonderful! But let's not punish ourselves with this. Instead, let's open our hearts and welcome meditation with non-judgemental acceptance – the very things meditation helps us achieve.

Meditation's benefits are well known and varied, from relaxation to resetting our nervous system. Although these are great outcomes (and really are a great argument for meditation), this is not why I'm including meditation as its own chapter. No, I include meditation because it enforces stillness, space and silence – exactly where your answers can be heard. **Meditation is the embodiment of receiving.** When meditating specifically to seek guidance and insight, rather than just the relaxation benefits, you really can go beyond your mind.

Meditating for Guidance

By now, we know that receiving answers and Universal guidance requires setting our vibration according to what we want the Universe to match. We know minds left to their own busyness won't attract the kinds of answers our hearts desire. And the more we practise allowing and receiving, the more we can actually receive. Meditation, then, provides some great assistance to our quest, because meditation:

- ♥ slows the mind's chatter and decreases the noise

- ♥ drops you into your heart space

- ♥ brings awareness to your inner state (or vibration)

- ♥ helps set the vibration of the answer or solution you seek (expanding your heart's desire)

- ♥ creates a state of receiving.

The Law of Compensation will reward the stillness, space and silence, if not just through a sense of calm and inner peace, then also through reams of intuitive data via our heart's desires, sensations in our Four Bodies, recognising the thoughts on repeat in our mind and awareness of our inner state. All this comes to the surface when we meditate for guidance, feeding back data for internal realignment.

Different forms of meditation can be deployed depending on our intention or the nature of the question. The following pages cover meditation tools for each of the Four Bodies, but you may see benefit in using them for other intentions too.

Mental: Mindful Meditation

More traditional and rather formal meditation techniques create states of transcendental awareness, mindfulness or inner peace, often born out of cultural or religious tradition. As such, these techniques deserve respect; we don't want to change these practices, but instead work with them. Many of these practices work with mantras, chanting, focal points like candles and pictures to focus the mind and reduce its chatter. By reaching a transcendental state, higher and inner guidance can be heard.

Beyond formal meditation techniques, a simple practice of following your breath in through the nostrils, pausing, then following the breath as it passes out through your nostrils again is a simple meditative technique that can help still the mind and rest the nervous system. Guidance may not necessarily arrive with the practice itself, but it can set you up for more of your morning ritual or reset you during the day, bringing you back to your heart.

While meditation helps *clear* the mind, mindfulness helps *focus* the mind, easing the mental load. As each thought enters your mind, imagine it floating on a cloud, gently and effortlessly passing through your mind. Mindfulness encourages true presence in your day and in the activity before you, allowing you to offer your full essence in the moment. Approach everyday moments like making a cup of tea, brushing your teeth or showering with a mindful presence, as explained in the exercise below. Such techniques bring you out of a rushing mind into the body and heart, to whole-heartedly feel and experience the moment you are in. After all, it's the only moment you ever really have.

Whatever technique you explore, for our purposes with receiving guidance, maintain your observer role of non-attachment (which is precisely what these techniques are designed to instil).

EVERYDAY MINDFULNESS

Everyday activities are an opportunity to practise mindfulness. Try mindfully making a cup of tea:

1. Focus as you fill the kettle, listening to the running water, feeling the weight of the kettle increase as it fills with water.

2. Turn the kettle on. When it gets hot enough, listen to the water bubble and boil.

3. Notice when your kettle signals it has reached the ideal temperature.

4. Mindfully place the tea in your cup or pot. Gently pour in the hot water. Smell the fragrance of the tea leaves, watch the colours swirl as the tea releases them into the water.

5. Witness the steam rising off the top of the cup, the warmth in your hands as you hold your cup, the warm liquid hitting your tongue, passing along your throat and warming your belly.

What does it feel like to be so present to such a simple activity? Record this in your journal (while enjoying your cup of tea!).

Spiritual: Guided Meditation

One of the best ways I learned to connect with my heart and intuition was through guided meditations. Before long, I was guided to create my own, which are available on my website. Guided meditations are a specific practice leading the listener through a visualisation (great for focusing busy minds) and including a series of questions or experiences where symbolic answers may arise. These meditations can be recorded, or someone can guide you through them in real time. Some meditations will help you pose a question during the meditation, or you may need to set your intention beforehand (remember, we must ask to receive). Be sure to record all impressions in your journal after the meditation, and interpret them. Listening to guided meditations will often give rise to colours, imagery and symbols in your mind's eye, giving you plenty of clues to interpret via the tools in Chapter Five.

Like oracle cards, not all guided meditations are created equal. You can find guided meditations to relax, open your heart, clear your energy, raise your vibration, connect with your intuition and guidance, and more. You may be intuitively drawn to different meditations or want to find ones designed for the particular life area your BSQ is linked to.

Physical: Meditating on the Body

Sitting quietly for a few minutes and mindfully scanning your body is a powerful meditative practice. Intend to bring all your awareness to your body and ask it to reveal its wisdom, then observe what's present. What you discover will now prompt supporting questions to understand how these sensations and emotions can be processed. Ask each sensation what it represents. What does the body part represent to you? You may be surprised by the intuitive answer that arises. Bringing breath to these parts of your body can help ease tension and stress, and also help to move along any stagnant energy stored there. It's not unusual for tears to flow during such a practice.

Emotional: Meditating on Emotions

Emotions can be overwhelming, particularly the uncomfortable ones. Ignored emotions tend to fester and, of course, some emotions are avoided for a reason. What I suggest here isn't meant to trigger or retraumatise anyone unnecessarily; such emotional excavation may require additional support from a therapist or qualified practitioner. That said, we can achieve a lot on our own, simply by following our hearts. When big emotions arise or need processing, try the exercise on the opposite page. The questions within also make great journaling prompts.

The insights received from the emotions present show us where the inner work should focus. **Emotions are a guiding force back into our highest vibration.** The Law of Correspondence ensures a festering emotion will eventually arise in one of the other Four Bodies, perhaps as a physical ailment, or as a block in our relationships or career. So if starting with the deeper emotional work is hard, know that working with the other bodies will have a knock-on effect.

MEDITATING ON YOUR EMOTIONS

Scan your Four Bodies, paying particular attention to the sensations in your anatomical body and the emotions that arise.

As emotions arise, sit with them, bringing breath into the area. Allow the emotion to be present. Don't avoid it or rush it. Notice how it feels in your body.

Hold the intention to sink further into this (possibly uncomfortable) feeling – then ask it why it is here. Allow an answer to arrive.

If more emotions arise, repeat the process, each time asking the emotion:

- ♥ What do you want me to know?

- ♥ When did you become stuck, stagnant or stored in my body? Why?

- ♥ What are you here to teach me?

- ♥ How can I transform you?

Allow emotions to be fully felt. They will eventually pass. Record all impressions in your journal.

Troubleshooting

Q: What if I can't sit still?

A: Try a moving meditation. In its purest form, yoga is meditation. The gentle movements are designed to limber up the body so you can sit for extended periods of time in a meditative state. In Chapter Ten, I introduce some other suggestions for moving meditation.

Q: What if my mind is too busy?

A: Try stream of consciousness journaling before you meditate (see page 102). Mind mapping may also help. More formalised meditations may be better suited to you, as mantras or focal points can steer your mind, giving it a task to focus on. Meditative music can also be beneficial. Simply sit with your earphones in, close your eyes, focus on your breath and listen.

Q: What if I don't have time?

A: Another confession: I don't meditate every day. Some days, I only manage to mindfully brush my teeth or meditate while in the shower. But it's not the norm and, thanks to the Law of Rhythm and the Law of Balance, I allow my practice to ebb and flow. That isn't always popular advice with the meditation crowd. If you don't have time on the odd occasion, that's ok … but I prompt you to check if it's your head or heart claiming that you lack the time. When truly stretched for time, try meditating sitting in bed as you prepare for sleep. If nothing else, it may assist with a deep, restful sleep, which, if you are truly that busy, is probably the guidance you'd receive anyway.

Q: What if I fall asleep during meditation, especially guided meditation?

A: I've had this feedback on my collection of meditations and I do not take it personally! In fact, it's a good sign. Your body is naturally doing what it needs to do when it receives those frequencies. High vibrational energy, such as what might be present during a guided meditation, works beyond the mental plane, bypassing the mind's logic – which is a lot easier if you're asleep! Trust that it's what you need at that time. If it persists, try other meditations (guided or otherwise), or perhaps a moving meditation would suit you better.

Still resisting meditation? Use this as an intuitive clue and take it to the ARIA Method.

Recap

- ♥ Meditating for guidance is about creating moments of stillness, space and silence so you can listen.

- ♥ You may like to practise formal meditation techniques, although many will suggest you stay unattached to the guidance you receive there.

- ♥ Depending on what you're experiencing or asking about, you may like to try different meditation techniques for your physical, mental, emotional and spiritual health.

♥ If meditation is still a struggle, work with mindfulness and presence instead.

♥ Record all your impressions from your meditations and interpret them.

♥ Take one of the suggestions here and add it to your daily ritual, knowing you can change it later.

CHAPTER TEN

EXPRESSION

Nearing the end of Part Two, we now explore the last tool in our toolkit: expression. At first glance, this chapter may seem out of place, but expression is one of the quickest shortcuts to our heart's guidance. Connecting with your heart and giving yourself permission to speak, move or play without censoring yourself allows surprising insights to emerge. Expression here is far more than verbal communication – it's an expression of energy, truth and essence as transmitted to the Universe through the heart. Creative self-expression reveals how the heart really feels and how the mind holds it back. Imagine what might happen if the heart could bypass the mind's censorship?

Introverts: no cause for alarm. No extrovert conversion required. Instead, this chapter offers some simple practices to loosen the mind's grip on your self-expression, explored in private, low-risk environments. The goal here is unearthing the heart's dormant desires through *intuitive* expression. New messages will arrive now via simple movement practices, working with your inner voice and exploring your creativity.

Exercises in this chapter can act as an antidote for those struggling with meditation. Energy has to keep moving (remember, it's Universal Law), so by letting it flow through creative self-expression, you can observe new meanings and insights, while also releasing stored emotions and transmitting a new frequency. Our expression offers us so much more, if we let it.

Movement

Physical movement isn't just beneficial to our health, but to our energetic body too. Movement puts life force energy into motion. Without it, energy pools, becoming stagnant and stuck, causing havoc across the other Four Bodies. *Intuitive* movement allows that life force energy to move through the bodies, to express, release and transform as it already knows how to do. Children don't censor themselves; they haven't yet learned how. So they dance when and how they want, they show their anger and frustration when and how they want, and they give themselves full permission to experience unbridled joy. Intuitive expression builds your capacity to experience your full range of emotions, tapping into your heart's truth. If you do have children, try this with them (and even if you don't, please try it for yourself).

Intuitive movement must be directed by the heart, not the head. The heart must be free to express itself without the mind's censorship. Movement without thinking. Allow your body to move freely, without thought. Energy will transform. Emotions will arise. And your mind will want to control it. At the very least, your inner critic will judge it.

Walking

Mindfully walking in nature is a perfect meditation alternative. But it means no distractions (no music, no chatting with a friend). Just you, alone with yourself, in nature. Longer hikes or a walk through local nature reserves could be built into your weekly or monthly practice (see the next chapter), but a brief daily stroll around the block is equally powerful.

Getting the heart rate up or hitting today's step target isn't necessarily our goal here (although it obviously has its own benefits). Walking meditation requires mindfulness. Notice your natural walking pace (and how the mind may want to change or manage it). Notice your breathing. Soak in the surroundings, the sights and sounds. Slow down to observe the trees, the wildlife. Sit under a tree and open your heart to it. Yes, I know how that sounds … but *try it*. You may just find a few new things to add to your daily gratitude list.

Yoga

In its purest, original form, yoga is a deeply spiritual practice in Hinduism, with similar practices in Buddhism, to help the yogi practice non-attachment and reach a higher state of consciousness. Traditionally, the physical poses limbered up the body to allow the yogi to sit for extended periods of time in transcendental meditation. As such, it is a deeply sacred practice and not to be confused with the Westernised versions you may be more familiar with. We can learn from this practice. There is a deep connection between the body, the mind and the spirit and a gentle awareness of this can bring us back into our centre, to hear our hearts once more.

Simple Mindful Stretching

An easy addition to your morning routine, this can be done as soon as you're out of bed, before you even dress. Close your eyes and tune into your body. How does it feel? What does it need? Then, without thought, allow yourself to stretch and bend or contort however your body guides you to. This isn't about perfecting a pose, but rather to allow yourself to freely move your body as you feel guided. During this practice, notice what else arises physically, mentally, emotionally and energetically. What do your physical sensations tell you? What emotions arise? Are you more connected to your body as a result? This is perfect to practise throughout the day, when the mind is racing or you feel ungrounded or disconnected.

Dance

Do not skip over the following exercise. It's one of the more powerful techniques for intuitive expression. But it's also potentially one of the most uncomfortable (which we now know is an important guidance clue).

Any form of dance will help you move energy through your body, but intuitive dance is far less about performing a set routine or taught steps than letting your heart take the lead. You could build up to this practice from the simple stretches mentioned above. Beyond stretching, intuitive dance means letting your body move – sway, jerk, fold – however it wants to. Truly dance like nobody's watching – because during this practice, they're not. Before you move on with your reading, I encourage you to try the technique in the box opposite. I imagine this is the exact point your mind will tell you, 'Oh, just read it. Do it in your head. You can come back to it later', as I suggested you might in the introduction. Please dance anyway.

EXPRESSIVE DANCE

1. Find somewhere quiet and private, where no one is watching or will disturb you.

2. Set a five-minute timer and complete the following steps until the timer goes off.

3. Without music, with your eyes closed if you prefer, begin to move your body in a gentle dance. This is about tuning into your heart and allowing it to guide your movement.

4. During this process, notice your mind's objections. Notice the thoughts and judgements. Notice the emotions. But keep going!

5. When the timer stops, so can you.

Record all the impressions – including resistance, objections and judgements – in your journal.

The first time I attempted this practice, I hid in my windowless bathroom with the door closed, even though I was already home alone. Even with my back to the mirror, my eyes closed, I felt incredibly self-conscious. But I did it anyway. As the timer went off, I had tears streaming down my face – it was truly one of the first times I gave myself permission to move and express without an internal judgement. What a liberation!

Voice and Sound

Voice and sound are synonymous with expression, but are far more powerful than you might expect. Your voice has its own resonance and frequency, as does music. Using your own voice, others' voices or the frequency of sound to clear, heal and restore your internal vibrations is a powerful way of releasing stored and stagnant emotions and for energy to flow and recalibrate internally. The 'om' chanted at the start and close of a yoga class, for example, is said to be the frequency running through all of creation. Bathing in the phenomenal sounds of crystal healing bowls is a convincing way to experience the power of sound (and if you haven't tried it, I highly recommend it).

If we want to change our internal vibration, our voice is one way to shift it, *fast*. We can use our voice to speak, sing, chant or even laugh and allow the resonance to do the work for us. Here are some ways you can use your voice to shift energy and listen to your own heart's vibration:

- ♥ **Chanting.** This may be done alone or with a group, or using a mantra.

- ♥ **Singing.** This one allows you to select a song you love, or lyrics you wish to express, and truly sing like nobody's listening.

- ♥ **Laughing.** Also likely to bring up some discomfort at first, it can be incredibly refreshing to force yourself to laugh … only to then laugh at yourself in the process. A great way to de-stress, if nothing else, and something I do with my kids when we need a diversion.

♥ **Sound baths.** This is more passive than using your own voice, but it's a powerful healing tool that uses sound frequencies to move and alter your vibrational state. Music will work as a sound bath, as will clapping and stomping. A great way to shift stagnant, trapped or heavy energy in your home or office.

When my children are in a bad mood, to shift it we will laugh, be silly, make funny sounds or the like. Not only does it get us giggling, but the bad mood and lower vibe evaporates too. When alone, intuitive singing (similar to the intuitive dance exercise above) harnesses the power of your voice to transmute energy and emotions, releasing them from your body, without the mind's interruption. This may be another one your head will fight against.

INTUITIVE SINGING

1. Find somewhere quiet and private, where no one is watching or will disturb you.

2. Set a five-minute timer and complete the following steps until the timer goes off.

3. Close your eyes if you prefer and place your awareness on your heart space. Feel your heart and allow yourself to make

whatever noise comes up and out. Just sound. This isn't about singing something you know, or holding a tune. It's about releasing the vibration that's stored within you. Yes, it may emerge as a guttural, visceral, even primal grunt. Trust the process.

4. Notice your mind's objections. Notice the thoughts and judgements. Notice the emotions. But keep going!

5. When the timer stops, so can you.

Record all the impressions – including resistance, objections, judgements – in your journal. With practice, you may also find you're recording emotions, and even healing.

My first attempt at this exercise unleashed deep, confronting guttural sounds. I stuck it out and by the end my voice had found its own melody, what I call my Soul Song. Again, the tears came as I heard the way my voice wanted to translate my energy. I will often do a version of this before speaking at an event or hosting a live webinar, clearing the way for my heart's wisdom and transmission to be shared with others.

Creativity

Not to be confused with artistic ability, we are indeed all creative beings connected to the same creative source through the Law of Divine Oneness. The Law of Perpetual Transmutation of Energy reminds us that energy is continually changing form, whether it's our thoughts changing into a physical form, or we turn ingredients into a cake, or take raw materials and turn them into a work of art. Our powerful creative life force can help us process our emotions, thoughts and experiences and transmit what's in our hearts when our minds and words cannot. When feeling creatively blocked, the exercises earlier in this chapter, especially the intuitive dance and intuitive singing, clear out stagnant, stale energy, creating room for fresh, creative energy to flood in (perfect for the clearing and healing phases of the Guidance Cycle).

For some, using the creative process is easier than journaling, and if that's you, now is your chance to experiment! Creativity can take many forms. For the purpose of connecting with our hearts, it may look like:

- ♥ doodling
- ♥ writing/journaling
- ♥ sketching
- ♥ painting
- ♥ cooking
- ♥ singing
- ♥ dancing.

As you've worked through this book, have you already received guidance that has steered you towards creative pursuits? Don't be too quick to dismiss it just because your mind may not appreciate how a seemingly unrelated creative endeavour is going to help you solve your BSQ. Maybe you've heard, or even said, something like this about creativity:

- ♥ 'It's pointless.'
- ♥ 'I'm not very good at it.'
- ♥ 'This isn't very productive.'
- ♥ 'Who'd want to see what I've created?'

Get creative anyway, especially if your heart leads you there. The heart may guide you to pursue creativity:

- ♥ for the sheer pleasure of it
- ♥ to change your vibration
- ♥ to heal beyond the mind
- ♥ to process and move emotions, thoughts and experiences
- ♥ so that you stumble upon the very thing that lights you up, showing you a new direction
- ♥ to restore your energy through pleasure, so you can manifest your desires.

Follow your heart's creative impulses. Follow any intuitive nudges or Universal signs to attend classes, to create, to experiment (perhaps this is your nudge!). Weave it into your days, weeks, months and years. Creative life force energy will flow into your being and like will attract like. Getting lost in creativity for creativity's sake aligns us with the Universal creative energy – the same creative energy that created all of life. Who wouldn't want that kind of vibrational alignment? Imagine if that became your dominant vibrational set point!

Express Like the Universe Is Listening

Not sure which type of expression to include in your morning routine? Ask for guidance and notice who or what turns up. These tools don't need to be used every day. Just draw on them when guided, or as part of your extended practice (see the next chapter for more on this). That said, there are some that can be woven into your daily routine. Walk on your lunch break. Spice up tonight's meal. Sign up for the nude life drawing class. Play with your kids. Experiment. Let your inner voice have a say and see where it leads you. More than anything else, the frequency of fun will become a more dominant attraction magnet. The Universe is listening.

To help you as you explore which tools you need, whether that's for expression, meditation, oracles or journaling, I've included a table at the end of the Part Two recap (page 158). Have this nearby for your daily ritual from here on in and intuitively select what you need each day. You're now ready to expand your daily ritual into a weekly and monthly (and beyond) practice.

Recap

- ♥ You have a powerful voice, and it is a tool for expressing and moving your vibration.

- ♥ You can change your internal vibration by using the frequency of sound, including your own voice.

- ♥ Observe the ways your mind may try to censor your creative self-expression. Use the ARIA Method to enquire into why and how you can process and change that.

- ♥ Take one of the examples of expression from this chapter and build it into your morning ritual.

PART TWO RECAP

♥ You now have four key tools (journaling, oracles, meditation and expression) with myriad techniques as part of your extensive toolkit. Draw on this toolkit as part of your daily ritual.

♥ Your day-to-day practice may ebb and flow, but keep the ARIA Method and some combination of tools in your morning ritual. Intuitively include a mix of these tools, ensuring there is some balance of journaling, working with oracles, meditation and expression each day.

♥ If your practice ebbs more than it flows, try not to judge it but reflect on why. This may become a supporting question to take through the ARIA Method.

♥ You are about to expand your daily ritual to include a weekly and monthly component, factoring in the ebb and flow and working with the Law of Rhythm.

♥ Your personal vibration and intentions affect the flow of answers and opportunities to you. Continue using the feedback loop to highlight inner work, then take it to your toolkit to process and act.

♥ Remember, avoiding any particular tool may also be a sign to explore the resistance.

♥ You're now ready to expand and further personalise your ritual in the next chapter.

Your Toolkit

Make this toolkit your own by intuitively experimenting and exploring, adding to it as you manifest and attract your own additional tools. Make a note of which tools are best for certain BSQs or supporting questions, inner work or manifesting.

JOURNALING	ORACLES
Daily recording and reflecting	Oracle cards
Gratitude practice	Tarot cards
Scan your Four Bodies	Affirmation cards
Interpretation index	Playing cards
Stream of consciousness writing	Bibliomancy
Automatic writing	Pendulums
Morning pages	Muscle testing
Future scripting	Dream interpretation
Point of view writing	Signs and symbols
Prompts	Messengers
Dream journaling	
Inner child journaling	
Gratitude journaling	
Visual or creative journaling	

MEDITATION	EXPRESSION
Head versus heart	Mindful nature walks
Expand the vibration of your heart's desire	Yoga
	Mindful stretching
Cloud technique	Intuitive dance
Focused breathing	Intuitive singing
Transcendental meditation	Chanting
Guided meditations	Singing
Scan your Four Bodies	Laughing
Emotional embodiment	Sound baths
Mindful nature walks	Voice
Mindful activity	Sound
Music	Music
Focal points (e.g. mantra, image, flame)	Create
	Have fun

PART THREE

THE RHYTHM

CHAPTER ELEVEN

RHYTHM AND RITUAL

The Law of Rhythm says all of life is in constant, effortless, fluid motion, at a rhythm and pace all of its own. Everything will change eventually, and cycle back again – even your daily ritual of listening to and following your heart. As we move through our final chapter, we work with this natural rhythm, catering for the ebb and flow of your practice (although keep watch on the mind to ensure it's not manipulating that ebb for its own gain).

With every exercise you've experimented with, applying the ARIA Method and the particular tools you are drawn to, you may have already witnessed the emergence of your own natural rhythm. If not, you'll work through it now. Exploring each new tool and technique, you may have found it near impossible to include them all as part of your daily routine – and that's ok. Rely on your own intuition to determine what mix of tools to include each day, beyond the basic practice of recording and interpreting your messages. Now we add a weekly and monthly component (and beyond!), to account for the natural rhythm at play.

At the end of this chapter, on page 174, you'll find a table – 'Your Guidance Practice – At a Glance' – which suggests what tools to use when. Consider this an inner work shopping list of activities to mix and match according to your own heart (and where you might be in the Guidance Cycle or your own personal journey at any given point).

Let's now put the final pieces of your rhythm and ritual together.

Daily Practice

To date, the daily ritual has allowed for a combination of journaling, oracles, meditation and expression, working with as much or as little time as you can afford. Your morning routine will focus on the asking, receiving and interpreting phases of the ARIA Method, with some clear actions for immediate application. Most will take time and more inner work and vibrational realignment through the Guidance Cycle, as revealed in day after day of continued practice.

If nothing else, a few minutes each morning is paramount to set intentions, ask for guidance and allow yourself to receive. Your antennas continue to receive throughout the day, so recording impressions and insights (and their interpretations) is key. When low on time, adjust the ritual to a few dot points in your journal, a very simple meditation (like the breathing technique) and an oracle card or two to focus the day. At other times, or when dealing with something a little deeper, you may want to allocate more time for tools that require it. By evening, the gratitude practice completes the ritual, along with any final recording of impressions and reflections before bed, if needed. This is also where you may ask for further guidance in your dreams.

Some days, this practice will feel easy; on others, it will not. Be curious about why. (Bonus tip: observe the phase of your menstrual cycle or lunar cycle, as there may be a link.) On the tougher days, allow the resistance to guide you. In the absence of any other intuitive data, this is the work for the day.

After all that intuitive work to build your routine, I now include a suggested outline for this morning routine. Yes, I could have delivered this up-front, but then you wouldn't have built that trust in yourself and your own heart. Your ritual may already look like this, or not. Tweak as your heart requires.

BUILDING A DAILY RITUAL

1. Dedicate a special, physical space for this practice. Store your journal, oracle cards, books and other tools here, along with any decoration, such as candles, essential oils, flowers or soft lighting. Ensure the space is distraction-free. Just like muscle memory, your body knows it's time for the practice when you arrive.

2. Set an intention and bring at least one question to your daily ritual. Over time, the questions will change, taking you further inward for deeper inner work and vibrational realignment.

3. Start the ritual with a few quiet moments, centring your awareness in your heart space. Observe your Four Bodies, asking what they need today. Can you honour that now? If not, set a reminder to return to that action throughout the day.

4. In your journal, record the date, question/s and intention for today's practice. Record any impressions from the Four Bodies. Add in a journaling tool here, if needed. (See Chapter Seven.)

5. After journaling, centre yourself in your heart again. Reconnect with the energy of your question and intention. Now you might introduce an oracle tool from Chapter Eight. Record and interpret the message (see Chapter Five), updating your interpretation index if needed.

6. Layer in a meditation tool or mindfulness activity. Remember to hold the intention or question for this practice too. Again, record any impressions after your meditation.

7. Is there anything else you intuitively need now? Reflect on the toolkit from page 158 and include anything else you might need or make a note to return to it.

8. Most days, you'll end your practice here, or you may decide to review the impressions during the sitting. Trust that insights and clarity will continue throughout the day (remember to set the intention for this!).

9. Give thanks for any messages and insights, and thank yourself for this self-care practice.

10. Go about your day, observing who and what shows up in response to your energy. Keep your journal nearby to make notes as needed, or to action any intuitive instructions.

11. Before bed, reflect and note anything you need to. Practise gratitude and invite guidance into tonight's dreams. Wake, and repeat this process.

Weekly Practice

As your daily practice ebbs and flows, the introduction of a deeper, once-a-week practice will consolidate and clarify your daily practice. This may fall on a weekend, or whenever you typically have more time. I love going to a local park for this, or a different part of the house, or even off on a solo day trip if time and circumstances permit. Consider how this may also help you hit your creativity and fun quota.

Much like the daily ritual, the extended weekly practice expands the time spent on longer journaling practices, or a specific guided meditation or oracle card spread. It's about extending your pocket of time to receive. Use it wisely.

During this extended weekly practice, review your daily journal entries, looking for patterns, themes, symbols and connections across the days. Complete an extended daily practice, this time exploring the BSQ more deeply, or diving into the supporting questions for the specific clearing, healing or restoring required. You may just sit with your heart's desires longer than usual. Perhaps there are Inspired Actions from your daily practices that need extra time to complete. This may include an appointment with a therapist, healer or other practitioner you've been guided to work with.

While the day-to-day practice helps us with the daily intuitive instructions, these longer sittings can really help us understand the threads of healing and overarching direction, putting the Inspired Action into – well, action. The extended weekly ritual is a time for setting intentions for the week ahead, or even intuiting what the week ahead may hold (perhaps writing from the point of view of the future you, a week from now). Such intuitive predictions are great to revisit a week later, to see how they panned out.

Monthly Practice

Once a month, the focus moves towards even deeper reflection, building momentum and clarifying your direction. From this reflection, proof emerges of hunches and messages that have come to fruition. Sometimes this reflection will steer you towards re-interpretation. Such a monthly perspective teases out the overarching themes, zooming out on the picture to gain perspective and see what's lurking in the periphery. The mind will be appeased as it sees how your predictions panned out and how your manifestations materialised.

No need to find more time – just take the weekly practice towards the end of the month and either extend the time or change the intention for the sitting. Close the loop on anything that's been swirling and can now be let go of before setting an intention for the month ahead. Then pick up again tomorrow with your regular daily practice.

And Beyond

Don't stop there! Consider any other rhythm that makes sense for you. I check in quarterly and annually, and have also worked with my birthday, moon cycles, menstrual cycle and Mother Nature's seasons. Bigger milestones are a perfect time to revisit your future scripting from Chapter Seven. Let your heart guide you to the timing and frequency – just keep up the daily practice. As the years roll on, you'll gain another perspective to your rhythm and rituals.

Deepening the Process

Over time, the feedback loop weaves into your daily, weekly and monthly practice, allowing both the manifestation of your desires *and* the guidance to realign them, or yourself, for greater success. The feedback loop catalyses inner transformation, realignment and recalibration, so we can manifest what's a match for our internal state. Your daily, weekly and monthly practices (and beyond) allow small changes over time. While the prospect of following your heart and intuition may have seemed overwhelming, you've now broken it down into smaller, actionable daily steps that add up to significant change – inside and out.

Both intuition *and* manifesting are required (Law of Polarity) as we exchange vibrational information back and forth (Law of Balance) in co-creation with the Universe, seeing ourselves as part of the whole of life (Law of Divine Oneness), constantly evolving (Law of Perpetual Transmutation of Energy) in response. We will attract to us from the Universe (the Law of Attraction) prompts for inner action, change and transformation. We may intuit that an old belief needs reframing, or an emotional wound needs tending, or that stagnant energy needs to move to unblock the creative expression of a higher vibration.

Following this guidance, you continue to clear, heal and restore your energy, realigning your vibration so you can indeed manifest (and attract to you) what your heart desires. **Your heart showed you what you really wanted, and how to get it.**

What started as a head-based BSQ has been reworked into an introspective line of questioning to clear, heal or restore your Four Bodies. With continued rhythm and ritual, the questions become far more inward-focused, leading to greater self-awareness. With each practice, you deepen the feedback loop. You ask, receive, interpret and act to see outer world manifestations, which again prompt inner world reflection through more asking, receiving, interpreting and acting. On and on it goes – the Law of Rhythm says so. Through the Law of Correspondence, you deepen your relationship with self, your relationship with others and your relationship with life itself. The Universe will compensate you for your willingness and courage.

The Inner Work

We started this book with a focus on following your heart and intuition which, as Steve reminds us, somehow already know who you truly want to become. This process is not just a shortcut to some happy-ever-after. It's a neat internal navigation system whose primary function is to serve our personal growth and align us with our own divine life path. This was the premise of my first book, *You Already Know*. Chances are, as you commit to this process you'll be guided deeper and deeper to yourself, into a rabbit warren of inner work.

Continued use of this practice will deliver you far more guidance towards your inner healing (thanks to the healing journey thread, from our discussion of the Three Threads of Guidance from Chapter Six). This will prompt a great deal of inner work, frustrating the mind, which just wants to fix, solve and change the outer world experience *instantly*. The heart has a timing and a rhythm all of its own. You can work with its transmissions and received signals to attract and find the teachers, classes, events, books, workshops and additional tools not only for your inner healing, but for manifesting a life true to you.

The deeper we go internally, the deeper the corresponding outer world experience. With time, those smaller daily rituals will build momentum, gaining traction with some very big changes in perspective, vibration and your outer world. With time and consistent practice, these tools will overhaul your life, from the inside out.

Moving through the phases of inner work and healing, more of the overarching direction thread reveals itself to us. New meaningful connections arise, new ways of expressing and sharing ourselves with the world arrive, and our guidance begins to prompt the creation, sharing and transmission of who we really are, on purpose. Then our best life will indeed have manifested – and our heart will be able to truly enjoy it.

Follow Your Heart's Rhythm

How do you want to personalise your weekly and monthly routine? Let your heart feel into the best rhythm for you, then hand it to your head to plot and plan, allocating time in your calendar for the extended practices, or even making a note of the moon calendars. (If you work on a Google calendar, there is a moon phase extension you can add straight into your calendar. Handy!)

A sample routine is provided on page 174. Always work with your heart's natural rhythm and what it needs at any moment.

Your Guidance Practice – At a Glance

RHYTHM	RITUAL	TOOLS	TIME
Daily	Morning	Journaling Meditation Oracles Expression	Minimum 5 minutes, up to an hour if time permits. Let it ebb and flow.
	Throughout the day	Observing and recording	A few minutes, as required
	Evening	Gratitude practice Reflection	5–10 minutes
Weekly	Extended practice	Reflection Intention-setting Journaling Meditation Oracles Expression	An hour is ideal, longer if time permits
Monthly	Extended practice	Reflection Intention-setting Journaling Meditation Oracles Expression	An hour is ideal, longer if time permits
Beyond	Extended practice	Reflection Intention-setting Journaling Meditation Oracles Expression	A day is ideal

POTENTIAL QUESTIONS	POSSIBLE EXERCISES

What do I need to know today for my personal/inner growth?
How does my heart feel today?
What does my heart need today?
What do I need to take care of myself today – physically, mentally, emotionally and spiritually?
Where can I bring myself back into alignment?
What small steps can I take today to bring alignment?
	Head versus Heart exercise
	Expand the Vibration of Your Heart's Desire
	BSQ and supporting questions
	Record and review
	Add interpretations to index
	Select from:
	Journaling techniques
	   • oracle tool
	   • meditation techniques
	   • expression tools
	   • take Inspired Actions on daily intuitive instructions

What do I need right now? What do each of my Four Bodies need right now?	Head versus Heart exercise Expand the Vibration of Your Heart's Desire Listen to your Four Bodies Notice messengers, signs, symbols Add interpretations to index Have fun/create/express
What am I grateful for today? What guidance or healing do I need in my sleep?	Gratitude practise Ask for guidance in dreams

Who or what am I ready to let go?
What am I healing?
Where do I need to restore?
What does my heart truly want me to create more of in my life? How?
What patterns and themes are present this week?
What tool do I need to draw upon from my toolkit?
	Daily practice plus …
	Explore feedback loop
	BSQ and supporting questions
	Deeper practices:
	   • journaling • oracles
	   • meditation • expression
	Identify your Inspired Actions
	Take action
	Weekly intention-setting

How is this current challenge in my life serving me? How can I grow from this situation? What do I need to let go of, or heal, inside myself to improve this situation? How can I bring a new perspective to this area of my life?	Weekly practice plus … Repeat the ARIA Method for inner work Future scripting Monthly reflection Monthly intention-setting
Any of the above questions	Monthly practice plus … Repeat the ARIA Method for inner work Future scripting Reflection

FINAL THOUGHTS

As I was preparing to submit the first draft of this manuscript to my publisher, another rather large carpet python appeared on the roof of my home studio (and was promptly caught by a professional snake-catcher and humanely relocated). Intuitively, I knew the snake signalled the shedding of another 'layer of skin', a change or rebirth of sorts as I completed writing this book. A quick Google search told me the snake also signalled spiritual guidance and the manifestation of new energy. The Universe, it seems, has a sense of humour. And perhaps I still need to reset the vibration I have for attracting snakes.

Following our heart and co-creating a life we love with the Universe can feel like a radical act. Rebelling against societal or familial norms, re-conditioning our programming and allowing ourselves to *feel* is liberating. It's not for the faint-hearted. But it can also be humorous, surprising and abundantly miraculous. And, depending on which viewpoint you align with, you will attract more of that to you too.

When I first followed my heart out of PR and into giving psychic readings, I had no real way of logically knowing what lay ahead. I had a feeling – a hunch – it would be pretty good. And it was. Still is. But that doesn't mean it's smooth sailing every day. Quite the contrary – a willingness to be guided into the inner work means things can get messy and hard and all too real. But life will throw that to you regardless of how you approach it. Following your heart and working with Universal Laws means you can weather anything that comes your way (and understand how you may have contributed to the weather pattern to begin with). Your heart can keep you grounded and centred when all else around you swirls. And this crazy adventure can remind you to be grateful you are even having this adventure to begin with!

No amount of willpower will manifest something that is out of alignment with your heart. This process won't guarantee you permanent happiness or riches or opportunities your mind *thinks* it needs to solve your problems. This isn't about becoming the next Steve Jobs. In fact, **this process is about becoming who you were always meant to be.** This process is about self-awareness, self-responsibility and self-actualisation. It's about understanding who you really are then living in accordance with that, wholeheartedly. It gives permission to those around you to do the same.

Following the beat and rhythm of your heart and intuition, however risky or unfamiliar, delivers life-changing benefits – and not just for the heart-led, but for all those around them. Imagine a world in which we never had music, cameras, memories, connection, entertainment and knowledge all bundled into a device at our fingertips, let alone the expanse of possibilities that opened up with its technology. Imagine if our mate Steve hadn't been courageous enough to follow his heart and intuition – how many of us may not have been able to fulfil our own dreams, or even had them ignited to begin with? What I hope you see now is: **we follow our hearts for us. The legacy is what becomes possible for others when we do.**

Imagine the world we might live in if we were all heart-aligned, working to bring our vibration into a higher frequency. We could literally change our planet – and the Law of Correspondence supports this idea. As every one of us works to increase our personal vibration, we will raise the collective consciousness of our planet, bringing healing to our world. That's how powerful this practice is, and our hearts are.

But don't just take my word for it. Or Steve's. Ask *your* heart. Ask your heart what kind of world it wants to create. Ask your heart how it wishes to contribute to that world. Ask your heart what ideas, talents and gifts are buried inside you, waiting to be unearthed and transmitted to the world. Your heart already knows these answers – it's always known who you are here to become, it's just been waiting for you to be courageous enough to ask. And follow where it leads.